OCS Study MMS 2005-041

Final Report

Trace Metals and Hydrocarbons in Sediments of the Beaufort Lagoon, Northeast Arctic Alaska, Exposed to Long-term Natural Oil Seepage, Recent Anthropogenic Activities and Pristine Conditions

Principal Investigator :   A. Sathy Naidu
Institute of Marine Science
University of Alaska
Fairbanks, AK 99775
<ffsan@uaf.edu>

Co-Principal Investigator: John J. Kelley, Institute of Marine Science
University of Alaska
Fairbanks, AK 99775
<ffjjk@uaf.edu>

Co-Principal Investigator: Debasmita Misra
School of Engineering and Mines
University of Alaska Fairbanks
Fairbanks, AK 99775
<ffdm1@uaf.edu>

And: M. Indira Venkatesan
Institute of Geophysics and Planetary Physics
University of California,
Los Angeles, CA 90095-1567
<indira@ucla.edu>

January 2006

Table of Contents

List of Figures

List of Plates

List of Tables

ABSTRACT

There is a concern that anthropogenic contaminants discharged during petroleum-related activities can accumulate in the Beaufort Lagoon sediments. In response to this concern, concentrations of 12 metals were analyzed [copper (Cu), chromium (Cr), cadmium (Cd), nickel (Ni), vanadium (V), lead (Pb), tin (Sn), zinc (Zn), arsenic (As), barium (Ba), iron (Fe), and manganese (Mn)] in the mud fraction and total mercury (THg) and hydrocarbons [saturated compounds such as normal and isoprenoid alkanes, triterpanes, steranes and polycyclic aromatic hydrocarbons (PAHs)] determined in gross sediments collected at 22 locations at the lagoon and in one natural oil seep.

The concentrations of the metals and hydrocarbons are generally lower than those reported for polluted marine sediments. Comparison of time-interval metal data on sandy mud (>75% mud) and mud collected in 1977 and 2003, respectively, shows a significant decrease in vanadium but an increase in manganese and copper from 1977 to 2003. Presumably, the differences are ascribed to disparities in the granulometry of the two sediment sets. Correlation coefficient analysis suggests that most metals are co-precipitated with iron oxy-hydroxide or occur as metal-organic complexes. There was a net increasing southeast to northwest trend in the metal concentrations, which did not relate to a possible gradient from point source such as the natural oil seep or the Distant Early Warning (DEW, now defunct) line station.

The hydrocarbon components in the sediments are essentially of terrestrial and biogenic sources with undetectable petroleum inputs, which is supported by the Organic Carbon to Nitrogen ratio (OC/N), isotope ratios of organic carbon ($\delta^{13}C$) and nitrogen ($\delta^{15}N$) of organic matter. There is no evidence of the contribution of petroleum hydrocarbons to the lagoon sediments from the onshore oil seeps. The overall composition of the hydrocarbon profiles is very similar to those found in our previous studies in the sediments from Elson Lagoon and near-shore regions of the Colville Delta–Prudhoe Bay–Canning Delta. We saw no impression of the natural oil seep and anthropogenic activities on the sediment trace metals and the hydrocarbon profile. The metal and hydrocarbon data will serve as a baseline, which will be critical for ecological risk management of the North Slope in the context of contaminant inputs, and in the better understanding of the inorganic and organic geochemistry of Arctic sediments.

Plate 1: Dr. Naidu pointing at the oil seep discovered south of Nuvagapak Point, Beaufort Lagoon.

Plate 2: Dr. Kowalik in front of the ice-infested coast bluff with peat deposit eroding.

BACKGROUND/RELEVANCE TO FRAMEWORK ISSUES

The North Slope of Arctic Alaska, consisting of the Coastal and Foothill Provinces north of the Brooks Range, and the contiguous nearshore zone are oil- and gas-bearing regions, which have a high potential for commercial reserves. During the past 30 years, gas has been extracted from the western sector of the North Slope (NPRA) to supply the energy needs of Barrow. The Prudhoe Bay field has been the focus of petroleum production in the North Slope region. More recently, a number of subsidiary onshore and offshore oil prospects on the central North Slope adjacent to Prudhoe Bay have either been opened for operation (Alpine, Kuparuk, Milne, Northstar, Endecott) or are at various stages of consideration for development (Liberty Prospect). As part of the forthcoming oil and gas development, the U.S. Department of Interior's Minerals Management Service (MMS) has proposed lease sale 186 scheduled for 2003, sale 195 scheduled for 2005, and sale 202 scheduled for 2007. At this point, all the sales would cover the same general area, and the latter two would re-offer unleased blocks. Further, all three blocks extend beyond three miles offshore (within the Federal jurisdiction north of the barrier island), extending approximately four to twenty miles seaward of the OCS boundary that begins three miles from the coast.

The Arctic National Wildlife Refuge (ANWR), particularly the 1.5 million acre coastal plain, which has potential petroleum reserves (titled the 1002 area), is one of the most contentious areas for oil drilling, because of the presence of a variety of wildlife habitats (Douglas et al., 2002).

The petroleum-related developmental and production activities (drilling, marine and onshore coastal traffic, and housing) and associated enhanced urbanization of the native villages close to the 186, 195 and 202 lease sale areas are bound to impact the nearshore environment of the North Slope, as suggested by the consequences of similar activities elsewhere in the adjacent coastal region. A likely result is the discharge of industrial and municipal effluents (mud, fluids and formation cuttings associated with drilling, dredging operations, sewage and garbage disposal and traffic emissions) laced with toxic trace metals and hydrocarbons into adjacent waters and/or on ice. Although all of the above cited lease sales are in the offshore region, it is probable that any anthropogenic contaminants discharged will be entrained in the littoral (alongshore) currents and transported inshore into the lagoons. There is also the possibility of accidental spilling of crude into the lagoons. Plans are to transport offshore crude by submarine pipeline to the shore via the lagoons. In the lagoons the particle-reactive contaminants can be subsequently concentrated in sediments by adsorption, ion exchange and organic complex formation, and/or physical co-deposition of the fine-sized effluent particulates with mud in the relatively low-energy lagoon environment.

That concentrations of trace metals in sediments of the Alaskan Arctic can occur as a result of the discharge of drill cuttings and mud is documented in field experiments conducted in Prudhoe Bay (Northern Technical Services, 1981), in the Canadian Beaufort Sea shelf (Macdonald, 1982) and by the investigations of Snyder-Conn et al. (1990) following drilling operations at three sites around Stefansson Sound, north Arctic Alaska. These studies demonstrated that the persistence of Ba, Cr, Pb and Zn, and elevated levels of Al (elements typically associated with drilling effluents) occurred in sediments around the discharge sites. Elsewhere, for example in Campbell, Australia, the impact of exploratory offshore drilling on benthic communities has been demonstrated (Currie and Isaacs, 2005). More recently, Naidu et al. (2001, 2003a), based on 30 years of time-series monitoring of contaminants, showed a significant increase in Ba and V in sediments of the Beaufort Sea nearshore from 1977 baseline values to values reported in 1997 following oil development activities. Thus, the lagoon sediments of the North Slope, if they were to be the ultimate sink for both organic and inorganic anthropogenic chemicals, could be a major source of contaminants for benthic animals, as well as organisms which have a close link with sediments and which serve as transfer pathways of contaminants to higher trophic levels (Long et al., 1995, 1998; Thompson et al., 1999; Valette-Silver, 1999; Krantzberg et al., 2000; Lee et al., 2002; Mucha et al., 2005). The role of contaminated marine sediments as a source of toxic metals and hydrocarbons to benthos has been documented in many case studies (refer to an excellent summary in Weis et al., 2004). Environmental contamination is of particular concern in the Arctic where marine organisms being lipid rich, having a relatively simple and short food chain and low biodiversity, are vulnerable to bioaccumulation of toxic metals.

In response to the continued concerns for the fragile environment of the north Alaskan Arctic, especially in the context of the pending lease sales scheduled by MMS in 2003–2007 (tracts 186, 195 and 202), we have extended our investigations (Naidu et al., 2001; 2003a) to establish baselines on trace metals and hydrocarbons in the sediments of the Beaufort Lagoon (Fig. 1; a map showing the study area within ANWR is illustrated in Fig. 2). Other investigations of a similar nature in the North Slope nearshore are those of Sweeney (1984), Sweeney and Naidu (1989), Trefry et al. (2003) and Naidu et al. (2003b) on trace metals and those of Steinhauer et al. (1992) on hydrocarbons. We contend that the chemical baseline data established on nearshore sediments from elsewhere in the North Slope (Colville Delta–Prudhoe Bay–Barter Island and Elson Lagoon; Naidu, 1982, Naidu et al., 2001, 2003a and references therein) cannot be extrapolated to the Beaufort Lagoon and the adjacent nearshore region east of Barter Island. The Beaufort Lagoon, which is located at the remote eastern margin of the north Alaskan Arctic coast and far from intense industrial activities (Fig.2), has an environmental setting that sets it apart from lagoons located in the eastern and central North Slope. For example, the Beaufort Lagoon (unlike the latter lagoons) is backed by the lower slopes of mountains extending close to the water margin. Consequently, the rivers opening into the Beaufort Lagoon are of relatively higher competency and presumably have coarser sediment bedload. As the dispersal of the sediments is contained within a relatively closed basin with limited marine access, the lagoon can be an effective trap for the accumulation of sediment-borne contaminants. A unique feature of the Beaufort Lagoon region is the frequent piling up of sea ice against the seaward barrier beach, even in summer, with ice fragments set floating in the lagoon. Additionally, the Beaufort Lagoon consists of three contrasting environments: two of them, Angun Point in the northwest and Nuvagapak Point around a landing strip (Fig.1) have been subjected locally to long-term natural oil seeps (Plate 1) and recent military activities, respectively. The latter activities were related to a defunct Distant Early Warning (DEW) line station, and an airstrip, which is still active (Fig.1). The activities involved land vehicular, marine boat and aircraft operations. Presumably, these and related operations exposed the lagoon region adjacent to the station with refined petroleum products and metal contaminants, which are possibly lingering in sediments. The rest of the lagoon presumably has remained pristine. It is anticipated that the chemistries of the sediments from these diverse environments will be significantly different and will be in contrast to sediments that are known to be exposed to more recent and fresh petroleum input. For example, the sediments exposed to hydrocarbons from natural oil seeps will likely consist of weathered crude oil enriched with tar and other heavy hydrocarbons, those from Nuvagapak Point of refined oil products, and those from the pristine lagoon of hydrocarbons derived from natural biogenous (terrigenous and marine) sources with little or no petroleum input. In the case of sediments that are exposed to recent petroleum contamination, there will invariably be a predominance of unweathered crude, relatively enriched with lighter hydrocarbons. Thus, a difference in composition and concentration of trace metals in sediments, reflecting influence by the different sources, can be anticipated.

This report presents the highlights of a two-year study (2003–2005), which has as its major objective the measurement of the concentrations of a suite of 12 trace metals [copper (Cu), chromium (Cr), cadmium (Cd), nickel (Ni), vanadium (V), lead (Pb), tin (Sn), zinc (Zn), arsenic (As), barium (Ba), iron (Fe), and manganese (Mn)] in the mud fraction (<63 μm size), and total mercury (THg), sediment grain size, organic carbon (OC) and hydrocarbons (normal and isoprenoid alkanes, triterpenoids and steranes and polycyclic aromatic hydrocarbons) in the gross sediments of the Beaufort Lagoon (Figs.1 and 2). The choice of the above metals and hydrocarbons is based on the fact that these chemicals are often present in drilling effluents, crude and petroleum development and production activities (Macdonald, 1982; Snyder-Conn et al., 1990; Neff, 2002). The purpose of this study was to close a gap in baselines for sediment metals and hydrocarbons for a remote region of the North Slope coast.

HYPOTHESIS AND OBJECTIVES

We hypothesize that the compositions and concentrations of trace metals and hydrocarbons in the sediments of Beaufort Lagoon vary between the sectors that have been exposed to long-term (prehistoric) natural oil seep (enriched in weathered crude), recent military activities of a former DEW line station (with the input of anthropogenic metals and refined petroleum products), and the pristine environment (no inputs from oil seep, crude or refined petroleum or anthropogenic metal contaminants).

The primary objective of this study is to distinguish the concentrations of 12 metals (V, Cr, Cu, Ni, Zn, As, Cd, Pb, Sn, Ba, Fe and Mn)

in the mud fraction (<63 μm size), and THg and hydrocarbons (polycyclic aromatics and saturated hydrocarbons such as normal and isoprenoid alkanes, triterpenoids and steranes) in gross sediments between regions of the Beaufort Lagoon that are presumed to be exposed to long-term natural oil seep, anthropogenic input of refined petroleum products and pristine conditions. The objective is also to establish current baselines on the above trace metals and hydrocarbons in sediments of the Beaufort Lagoon for the purpose of monitoring contaminants.

MATERIAL AND METHODS

Samples

In August 2003, sediment samples from the Beaufort Lagoon were collected at 22 selected stations (Fig.1; Table 1) spread over three sectors. The samples were collected from a Boston Whaler, using a Van Veen grab sampler. A suite of four sediment samples (BLO3-12, BLO3-13, BLO3-14 and BLO3-15) was collected east of Angun Point adjacent to a known onshore natural oil seep site (Lat. 69.918° N and Long. 142.395° W, personal communication, Jim Clough, July 31, 2003; refer also to USGS, 1983), and another suite (BLO3-20 and BLO3-4B) off an oil seep site (OS) discovered by us at the bank of a small stream located south of Nuvagapak Point (Fig. 1, Plate 1). We had intended to get closer to the shoreline at Angun Point to collect samples from that area, but it was not possible to navigate to

the Point because of the presence of extensive shoals in the region. A third suite of samples (BLO3-4, BLO3-4B, BLO3-18, BLO-19 and BLO3-20) was collected around Nuvagapak Point, a region that was impacted by military activities connected with a DEW line station (now defunct) and an active aircraft landing strip. A fourth suite of samples (BLO3-1, BLO3-3, BLO3-5B, BLO3-6B, BLO3-9, BLO3-9B, BLO3-10, BLO3-11A, BLO3-16 and BLO3-17) was obtained from east of the lagoon and up current of Nuvagapak Point, a lagoon sector that is presumed pristine. Table 1 shows the coordinates for the sample locations, fixed by a GPS.

The film of surficial sediment in contact with the metal sampler was discarded to minimize metal contamination. The remaining surface oxidized 2 to 4 cm portion of each of the grab samples was taken and split, using a Teflon spatula, into three sets of sub samples. Each of the splits was transferred into three separate I-CAM glass jars, two of which were prerinsed with acid- and deionized distilled water (for trace metal, grain size and organic carbon analyses) and the third jar pre-baked and the cap lined with aluminum foil (for hydrocarbon analysis). One set was sent to Dr. M. I. Venkatesan, subcontractor at the University of California, Los Angeles for hydrocarbon analysis. A second set was sent to the subcontractor Frontier Geosciences, Seattle for trace metal analysis. The third set was retained by the PIs for analyses of the grain size, organic carbon and nitrogen and their stable isotopes at the University of Alaska Fairbanks. All these sediment samples were stored frozen until analyses.

Laboratory Analysis

The methods for the analyses of trace metals and hydrocarbons on sediments were essentially the same as those adopted in previously funded CMI/MMS studies elsewhere along the North Slope nearshore (Crecelius et al., 1991; Steinhauer and Boehm, 1992; Naidu et al., 2001, 2003a). Therefore, we believe that the chemical data obtained in this study will be valid for comparison with the previous database established for the North Slope region.

A brief description of the methods follows. Twelve metals (V, Cu, Cr, Ni, Zn, As, Cd, Pb, Sn, Ba, Fe and Mn) were analyzed in the mud fraction (<63μm size) of the sediment samples and THg in gross sediment. The rationale for choosing the mud fraction for the above 12 metals and THg on the gross sediments has been discussed in our two previous CMI/MMS-funded studies on North Slope lagoon sediments (Naidu et al., 2001, 2003a). A 5-gram split of each sediment sample was suspended in deionized distilled water and the resulting slurry was sieved through a 230-mesh nylon screen to obtain the mud fraction. The mud was freeze-dried and pulverized using an agate mortar and pestle. A 0.5 gram aliquot of the dry powder was taken into a 140-ml Teflon bomb and digested in 25 ml of a high-purity concentrated acid mixture consisting of 7ml-HF +15ml-HNO3 + 3ml-HCl

in an oven at 130°C for 12 hours. After cooling to room temperature, the digest was diluted to 100 ml with water processed by a Milli-Q Ultrapur Water Purification System, and the diluted sample returned to its original bomb. The resulting solution was dried and then again dissolved in 10% HNO3 and made up to 29 ml by adding deionized distilled water. From the final solution the 12 metals listed above were analyzed using either a direct injection Zeeman graphite furnace atomic absorption spectrometer (GF-AAS), a Perkin-Elmer Elan 6100 quadrupole inductively coupled plasma mass spectrometer (ICP/MS) or a PSA Excalibur automated hydride generation atomic fluorescence spectrometer (for As, EPA method 1632). Total Hg (THg) was analyzed on a 0.01–1.0 ml aliquot of the solution retained in the bomb, following SnCl2 reduction and dual gold amalgamation pre-concentration, and using cold-vapor atomic absorption spectrometry (CVAAS) as outlined in Bloom (1992, 1999).

The QA/QC (quality assurance/quality control) protocol prescribed by the U. S. Environmental Protection Agency (EPA) and National Oceanic and Atmospheric Administration (NOAA) for metal analysis was followed. It consisted of determining analytical precision through replicate runs, checking analytical accuracy via analyses of two Certified Reference Materials (CRM), namely NIST 2709 and IAEA 405, analyzing spiked sample and reagent blanks, and using ultrapure reagents for all analysis. As in our previous CMI-funded investigations, the trace metal analysis was subcontracted to Frontier Geosciences Inc., Seattle, which in 1997 participated successfully in the NOAA/NIST (National Institute of Standards and Testing) round robin interlaboratory exercise NOAA/11 for certification of QA/QC. The National Research Council of Canada (NRCC) conducted this exercise. The rating for the Frontier Geosciences was good to excellent. The results of the QA/QC relating to trace metals on this study are presented and discussed elsewhere in the report.

The hydrocarbon analysis for n-alkanes, PAHs, triterpenoids and steroids was done on gross sediments and according to well-established methods (Venkatesan et al., 1980,

1982, 1987; Venkatesan, 1994). After thawing the frozen sample the wet sediment was spiked with the following surrogates: deuterated n-alkanes (for n-alkanes) and hexamethylbenzene, dodecylbenzene and deuterated terphenyl (for PAHs). After solvent extraction and separation into individual compounds by GC the alkanes were quantified using a flame ionization detector. Tricyclic, di- and pentacyclic triterpenoids and PAHs were measured by GC/mass spectrometry. As in our last two CMI/MMS-funded investigations (Naidu et al., 2001, 2003a) 24 PAHs were analyzed, as well as six additional PAHs, which are routinely analyzed by NOAA/NS&T (NOAA/National Status and Trends Program) for QA. Dr. M. I. Venkatesan, UCLA, to whom the hydrocarbon analysis was subcontracted, successfully participated first in 1992 and then in 1999 in interlaboratory round robin exercises conducted by NOAA-NS&T/NIST. The QA/QC results on hydrocarbons pertaining to this study are enumerated elsewhere in this report.

At the Institute of Marine Science, University of Alaska Fairbanks (IMS/UAF) laboratory, the sediment grain size distributions were analyzed by the sieve-pipette method (Folk, 1968). The purpose of this analysis was to gain understanding of the influence of granulometry on the concentrations of trace metals and hydrocarbons. The contents of organic carbon (OC) and total nitrogen (N) and their stable isotopes ($\delta^{13}C$ and $\delta^{15}N$) were determined at UAF, on carbonate-free mud, following the methods outlined in Naidu et al.

(2000) and using a Thermo Finnigan Model Delta Plus XP isotope ratio mass spectrometer (IRMS). The values of $\delta^{13}C$ ($^o/_{oo}$) are referenced to the V-PDB standard and those of $\delta^{15}N$ ($^o/_{oo}$) to air standard. The standard error of the isotope analysis is ± 0.2%.

Statistical Analysis

Statistical Analysis consisted of the determination of the correlation coefficients between trace metals, OC, N, and the silt and clay percents in the mud fraction, to deduce the geochemical partitioning of the metals in the mud analyzed. The comparison between two time intervals was obtained for the concentrations of selected trace metals in sandy muds (>75% silt and clay, after Naidu, 1981) collected in 1977, and mud of this study, using the student 't' test. Cluster analysis (Euclidean distances, Ward's linkage) was undertaken to identify grouping, if any, of stations based on the trace metal compositions surrounding the above two point sources and the pristine lagoon. This was followed by a principal component analysis of the trace metal data to correlate station group separation by cluster analysis with sediment variables. Surface trend analysis was conducted using trace metal data, granulometry and OC content to elucidate if there are any geographical gradient(s) in the individual sediment parameters and the metals from presumptive point sources; for example, the oil seeps and the abandoned DEW line station around Angun and Nuvagapak Points, respectively.

RESULTS

The percents of solids, gravel, sand, silt, clay and mud in gross sediments and organic carbon (OC) and nitrogen (N), OC/N ratios (weight to weight basis of OC and N) and stable isotopes of OC and N ($\delta^{13}C$ and $\delta^{15}N$) in the mud fraction of the individual samples are included in Table 1. In Table 2 are shown the concentrations (on a dry weight basis) of 12 metals (V, Cr, Mn, Ni, Cu, Zn, As, Cd, Sn, Ba, Pb and Fe) in the mud fraction and of total Hg in the gross sediments. Table 2 also provides the arithmetic and geometric means of the concentrations of the metals analyzed on the 21 samples and also the standard deviations and coefficient of variations (CV) of the analysis relative to each of the metals in the 21 samples analyzed.

The results of the QA/QC procedure for the trace metal analyses in reference to calibration verification, calibration blanks, spikes, replicate analyses (for precision determination), and assessment of the analytical accuracy based on Certified Reference Materials NIST 2709 and IAEA 405 are presented in Tables 3, 4, 5, 6, and 7, respectively. The correlation coefficients (r values) determined between the concentrations of silt, clay, OC, N and the 12 metals in the mud fraction are shown in Table 8. These correlations were determined by assuming the total percentage of silt and clay in the mud fraction to be 100%, and by prorating (recalculating) the silt and clay percents based on the relative percents of silt and clay in the gross samples. In Table 9 is shown the time-interval comparison for Beaufort Lagoon in the concentrations of selected trace metals on suites of muddy sediments collected in 1977 (Naidu, 1981) and mud sampled in 2003 (this study, Table 2). The concentrations of the *n*-alkanes, polyaromatic hydrocarbons, triterpanes and steranes in sediments are shown in Tables 10, 11, 12, and 13.

DISCUSSION

Sediment Grain Size, Organic Carbon (OC) and Nitrogen (N)) and Their Isotope Compositions

The Beaufort Lagoon has a mosaic of sediment types, consisting of sandy muds to muddy sands, with occasional gravel (Table 1). Sediments from stations BL03-4B, BL03-19 and BL03-20, have significant or predominant amounts of gravel (Table 1). The mud fractions of sediments, which were taken for trace metal, OC, N and isotope analysis, generally contain relatively higher contents of silt than clay particles. In the gross sediments, which were taken for Hg analysis, there are wide differences in the contents of sand relative to mud. We discuss later the possible control of granulometry on the concentrations of 12 metals in the mud fraction and Hg in the gross sediments.

Concentrations of organic carbon (OC) and total nitrogen (N) in the mud fraction of the Beaufort Lagoon sediments in this study (Table 1) are generally higher by a factor of 1.7 compared to the gross sediments from the Simpson Lagoon–Prudhoe Bay region and by a factor of 2.9 compared to gross sediments from the Beaufort Lagoon (Naidu, 1985). The higher content of OC in mud than in gross sediments is not surprising, because OC (tied with organic and clay mineral grains) is invariably co-deposited with hydraulically similar finer silt and clay (mud) particles and also that clay minerals concentrated in mud have the greater ability to adsorb organics. Coarser particles such as sand in gross sediments are generally not associated with organic particles of similar size and, therefore, their presence in gross sediments tend to dilute the OC contents.

The OC/N ratios, and compositions of stable isotopes of carbon ($\delta^{13}C$) and nitrogen ($\delta^{15}N$) in the Beaufort Lagoon sediments (Table 1) indicate that all the samples consist predominantly of OC/organic matter derived from terrestrial C_3 plant sources, with minor input, if any, from marine or macrophyte sources. This interpretation is based on the conclusions of very exhaustive investigations relating to the isotopic and OC/N signatures of the end-member sources of OC/organic matter (terrestrial, marine phytoplankton, sea ice algae and marine macrophytes) in the coastal region of the Alaskan and Canadian Beaufort Sea (Naidu et al., 2000; Macdonald et al., 2004). Results of our studies on the sources of OC/organic matter in the Beaufort Lagoon sediments are consistent with those reported for the above areas and, as discussed later, with the conclusions on the sources of organics in the lagoon sediments based on the hydrocarbon composition. It is suggested that the high input of terrestrial OC/organic matter into the Beaufort Lagoon, as well as lagoons of the contiguous coastal region, is due to the large supply of sediments derived from the peat-rich shoreline, which has among the world's highest coastal erosion rates, 2–10 m/y, (Naidu et al., 2000, Macdonald et al., 2004 and references therein).

Trace Metal Studies

Quality Assurance/Quality Control (QA/QC): The results of the calibration verification procedure (Table 3), consisting of, for each metal, the known initial calibration verification-true value (ICV-TV) and the ICV-Observed value (ICV-OBS) showed that the percentage ICV recovery (ICV-Rec) for all metals except Fe was at acceptable levels (close to 100%). Likewise the blank analysis (Table 4), based on initial calibration blank (ICB) and the continuation calibration blank (CCB) on several runs, indicate very low contamination from the chemicals used throughout the analysis. Further, with reference to the use of spikes (Table 5) run in duplicates, and based on the values of the mean concentration of an individual metal via replicate analyses of a sample (Mean), Spike true value (Spike-TV) and observed spike value, we show that the spike percent recovery is close to 100% for all metals except Fe and Ba. The

reason for the consistent poor showings for Fe and Ba is unknown, but perhaps reflects the inherent limitation of the use of the ICP/MS technique. The analytical precision (Table 6), as suggested by the relative percent difference (RPD) on duplicate analytical runs of two sediment samples, would seem to be excellent for all metals except Hg, in which case it is very good and at acceptable levels (< 25%). Likewise, the analytical accuracy (Table 7), determined via certified values (Cert. value), analyzed or Observed values (Obs. Value) of two Certified Reference Materials (NIST 2709 and IAEA 405) are again at accepted levels for all metals with reference to both the standards, except for Cr and Cd for CRM NIST 2709 and Fe and Sn for CRM. The above discussion indicates that the QA/QC for the trace metal analysis is generally very good to excellent and our data are of high quality.

Trace Metal Distribution Pattern: In the following we discuss the results of the statistical analysis on the trace metal concentrations and their distributions in the mud fraction. The high coefficient of variations (%CV) about the mean for all the 13 metals (Table 2) obviously indicate that there are wide inter-sample variations in the concentrations of all the metals, with relatively low variability (<15% CV) for V, Cr and Fe. The reason for the high inter-sample variability in the THg contents may be ascribed to the differences in the sand content in the gross sediments, and for the rest of the metals in the silt and clay contents within the mud fraction. The other possible reason could be the differences in the contents of organic carbon (a measure of organic matter) between sediments. Yet another reason could be the differences in the Mn and Fe contents between the sediments analyzed. It is to be expected that the greater the amount of clay size particles, Mn and Fe contents, and/or larger content of organic carbon (and by implication organic matter) in the mud fraction or gross sediments, the relatively greater the concentrations of metals. This concentration could result from several likely processes, such as adsorption of metals on clays, formation of organic-metal complexes by ligand bonding, and/or co-precipitation of metals with Fe and Mn oxy-hydroxides. That such a granulometric control on metal content is affected in the case of the Beaufort Lagoon mud is demonstrated by the significant (p< .05) positive correlations between all trace metals, except Cr and Ba, and the clay content. The positive significant correlations observed between all the trace metals and Fe, suggests that Fe as oxy-hydroxide has an important role in scavenging and accumulating the metals in the mud of Beaufort Lagoon. In this context, it is to be noted that all the 2–5 cm surficial sediments (portions analyzed for trace metals) showed, at the time of collection, a brownish ochre coloration distinct from the underlying gray layers, an indication that Fe in the mud analyzed is most likely present in an oxidized state. Additional detailed investigations on metal partitioning on sediments from Simpson Lagoon and Beaufort Lagoon (located east of the Colville Delta), based on sequential extraction techniques, further substantiate the role of Fe oxy-hydroxides in sequestering metals in the north Alaskan Arctic sediments (Sweeney, 1984; Sweeney and Naidu, 1989). Likewise, organic carbon and Mn in the mud (Table 8) to some extent bond selected few metals (Zn, Cd, As and Sn by OC, and Ni, Sn and Pb by Mn) by forming organic-metal or Mn oxide/hydroxide-metal complexation. This interpretation is consistent with our earlier conclusions on the partitioning of trace metals on lagoon sediments from a wide region off the North Slope coast, namely from the Colville Delta–Prudhoe Bay–Canning Delta area (Naidu et al., 2001 and references therein) and from an earlier study in the Beaufort Lagoon (Naidu et al., 1981; 2003b).

Further statistical treatment of the distributions of the trace metal concentrations in the Beaufort Lagoon mud are enumerated in the following:

Univariate distributions and tests for normality
Histograms, box-and-whisker plots and normal probability plots suggested that most metal concentrations were near-normally distributed, but there are a number of outliers for several of the metals (Figs.3 and 4). These are of concern in statistical modeling or hypothesis testing when normality is assumed. Outliers will have a strong influence on Pearson's correlations, cluster analyses and ordinations.

Observed outliers include:

Cd: 2 large values at stations BL03-19, and BL03-20

Cr: One low value at station BL03-4

Mn: One relatively large value at station BL03-4 and one large value at station BL03-17

Ni: Low value at station BL03-4, high value at station BL03-17 (and BL03-20?)

Pb: Large value at station BL03-17

Sn: Large values at stations BL03-17, BL03-19, and BL03-20

V: Low value at station BL03-4.

Based on outliers alone, several stations clearly stand out as unusual (Fig. 4). These are BL03-4, which has low concentrations of Cr, Cu, Fe, Ni, Pb, V, and Zn, and BL03-17, which is characterized by high concentrations of Cu, Mn, Ni, Pb, and Sn. Stations BL03-19 and/or BL03-20 have similarly high concentrations of some, but not all, of these metals (e.g. Sn, Ni). These two stations are easily identified as outliers in the multivariate analysis (cluster analysis, ordination, as follows).

Cluster analysis based on metal concentrations
A cluster analysis based on Euclidean distances clearly indicated the different metal concentrations at stations BL03-4 and BL03-17, which did not cluster with any of the other stations (Fig.5). These two stations had a very different sediment composition from most other stations with a very low percentage of silt in the mud fraction (< 3%). The remaining stations clustered into three groups. Only one of these groups (Group C, consisting of stations BL03-4B, BL03-19, and BL03-20) formed a geographically coherent cluster (Fig.6). Stations in group C were characterized by a relatively low percentage of silt in the mud fraction and a high percentage of organic matter. These stations contained relatively high concentrations of a number of metals such as Mn, Ni, Pb, Sn and Cd. Cluster A included the four westernmost stations near Angun Point, as well as a number of stations in the southeastern part of the lagoon. Cluster B consisted of the remaining stations in the southeastern part of the lagoon and also

10

included station 3, which was located immediately adjacent to the three cluster C stations. Cluster A and B were distinguished by differences in sediment composition with a higher percentage of clay in the mud fraction. Stations in cluster B had generally higher concentrations of all metals, although the differences in means were small for Mn, Ni, Cd and Cr. Figure 7 summarizes the clustering of stations based on metal concentrations.

Principal components analysis based on metal concentrations

Results from Principal Components Analysis (PCA) suggest that much of the variability in the metal concentrations (78%) can be accounted for by only two Principal Components (Fig. 8). The station clusters, identified in the cluster analysis, map well onto the PC ordination (Fig. 9) with a clear separation between clusters. Stations BL03-4 and BL03-17 are again identified as clear outliers in the biplot (Fig. 9).

The loadings for the first two PCs (Table 14) suggest that the PC 1 reflects the average concentration of all metals, with high concentrations corresponding to high values of PC 1. That is, metal concentrations tend to increase along the x-axis in Figure 9. The PC 2 contrasts Mn, Cd, and Sn with Ba. Large values of the second PC (above zero line in Fig. 9) correspond to high concentrations of Ba, while small values of PC 2 correspond to high concentrations of Mn, Cd, and Sn.

Correlations between PC 1/PC 2 and latitude / longitude / sediment composition

Table 15 presents correlations between PC 1 and PC 2 with latitude, longitude, silt (%) and OC (%). PC 1 is negatively correlated with latitude, implying that most of the metals (positive loadings on PC 1) decrease with latitude from southeast to northwest. PC 1 is also positively correlated with organic carbon content, reflecting a tendency for metal content to be higher at stations with high organic carbon content. This is also evident in the generally positive correlation between metal concentrations and organic carbon.

PC 2 is strongly correlated with the percentage of silt in the mud fraction, implying that Mn, Cd, Sn and Pb (metals that are negatively correlated with PC 2, see above) decrease with silt content, while Zn and Ba increase with mud content (this is also obvious in direct correlations between metal concentrations).

The above correlations are strongly influenced by the outlying stations (BL03-4 and BL03-17). Therefore, the correlations excluding those 2 stations were computed (Table 16).

After exclusion of the 2 "outliers", PC 1 was most strongly correlated with the proportion of silt in the mud fraction and the percentage of organic carbon. This implies a strong decrease in the silt fraction and an increase in the organic carbon along the x-axis in Fig. 9 (Group C > Group B > Group A). In contrast, the PC 2 is positively correlated with the silt fraction. Thus, the silt fraction increases along the y-axis in Fig. 9 (Group B > Group A > Group C).

Multiple regressions of PC 1 and PC 2 with latitude, longitude and sediment characteristics

PC 1: The model that best explained variability in metal concentrations (as reflected in PC 1) was a regression of PC 1 on the silt fraction and latitude (best model chosen based on Akaike Information Criterion (AIC)). The regression (Fig. 10, Table 17) captured 72% of the variability in PC 1 and also captured the strong decrease in PC 1 with the silt fraction and with latitude. While the silt fraction explained most of the overall variability, a significant effect of latitude on PC 1 remained after accounting for the effects of silt. This effect reflected a southeast-northwest gradient in metal concentrations that primarily separates stations BL03-10, BL03-12, BL03-13, and BL03-14 in the northwestern part of the lagoon (4 points on the lower right in Fig. 11) from the remaining stations.

The geographic gradient was confirmed by simple linear regressions of individual metal concentrations on latitude/longitude (rotated axis to reflect SE–NW direction), which showed significant increases ($p < 0.05$) from NW to SE in Cu ($t = 2.72$, $p = 0.016$), Zn ($t = 2.23$, $p = 0.041$), and Ba ($t = 2.90$, $p = 0.011$).

PC 2: The best model explaining variability in PC 2 was a simple linear regression on mud content, which explained 77% of the variability in PC2. After accounting for the effects of mud, there was no significant effect of latitude, longitude or other sediment variables. A "threshold" model that fits separate means at low and high mud concentrations fit slightly better (in terms of AIC) than the linear model (Fig. 12). Stations with low mud concentrations in the lower left of Fig. 12 were characterized by low values of PC 2, reflecting high concentrations of Mn and Sn and low concentrations of Ba. These included most of the stations in the northwestern part of the lagoon.

In summary, a PCA based on metal concentrations primarily separates stations with relatively high metal concentrations from stations with relatively low concentrations along PC 1 (56% of overall variability). PC 2 (23% of overall variability) contrasts stations that tend to be high in Mn, Cd, and Sn and low in Ba (Group C and stations BL03-4 and BL03-17) with stations that tend to show the opposite pattern (e.g. Group A). These differences in metal concentrations reflect both geographical differences and differences in sediment characteristics. In general, there was a tendency for total metal concentrations (PC 1) to decrease with the silt fraction and with latitude from S to N and to increase with organic matter content.

While much of the variability in metal concentrations was explained by sediment characteristics, a significant geographical gradient remained even after accounting for the effects of sediment composition on PC 1. This gradient reflects differences in metal concentration between the "pristine" southeastern lagoon (higher concentrations of most metals) and the northwestern part of the lagoon that is not explained by differences in sediment composition.

The trends of metal concentrations decrease from southeast to northwest across the study area. It seems clear, therefore, that there are no definite distributional patterns in the concentrations of trace metals in the mud of Beaufort Lagoon, especially in the context of the hypothesis that we had mooted at the start of the

project. We had predicted that there would be significant differences in the metal concentrations between the regions exposed to natural oil seep, anthropogenic activities such as those related to the defunct DEW line station and the pristine environment portions of the lagoon. The above gradient is opposite to what one would expect, considering the presumed contaminant sources. It is suggested that any of the 13 metals investigated that might have been input into the lagoon from the oil seeps and/or past military activities are dispersed so widely and are so diluted that the effect of the point sources of the natural and anthropogenic contaminants are not decipherable in the lagoon mud. In summary, there is no significant difference between mud collected from possible "impacted areas" and the pristine portion of the lagoon, suggesting that the lagoon has remained uncontaminated as far as the trace metals analyzed in this study.

It is noted that the mean concentrations of all trace metals in the mud fraction of Beaufort Lagoon are generally close to the levels reported by us on mud samples from the Colville Delta–Prudhoe Bay–Canning Delta region (Naidu et al., 2001). Further, the mean concentration of THg in the gross sediments of Beaufort Lagoon is significantly higher (mean: 57 ng/g) than in gross sediments of the above deltaic region (mean: 19 ng/g). This difference in Hg is probably due to differences in the natural input of Hg from the hinterland sources, a proposition that remains to be further investigated.

Time-interval comparison of the mean concentrations of metals

A comparison is shown in Table 9 of the mean concentrations of a selected six metals between 5 sandy mud (>75% silt + clay) and 21 mud samples, which were collected in 1977 and this study (2003) respectively from Beaufort Lagoon. A significant (p< .05) decrease in V and an increase in Mn and Cu are noted from 1977 to 2003, whereas no differences in the time interval mean concentrations in Cr, Ni and Zn are identified. The differences may be artifacts of the differences in the granulometry and organic carbon contents between the two sets of samples rather than metal pollution, as alluded to previously. It is to be noted that we have minimized the effect of granulometry by restricting the comparison to mean metal values on sandy mud samples of 1977 and mud samples in this study. The fact that there is no wholesale increase in the mean concentrations of all or most of the metals concerned is consistent with our earlier inference that the Beaufort Lagoon has remained generally a clean environment over the 26-year period (1977–2003), despite the fact that the lagoon had been subjected to past anthropogenic activities from the operation of a Distant Early Warning (DEW) Line station.

Predicting toxicity in sediments with numeral trace metal quality guidelines

The mean concentrations of selected trace metals in Beaufort Lagoon mud were used to determine their potential for adverse effects on resident marine benthic organisms, following the guidelines proposed by Long et al. (1995, 1998). Long et al., based upon empirical analysis of a broad database consisting of equilibrium-partitioning modeling, laboratory bioassays and field studies on total sediments have developed two sediment quality guideline (SQG) values [an effects range-low (ERL), and an effects range-medium (ERM)]. The database specifically consisted of concentrations of selected trace metals and hydrocarbons and biological effects on numerous benthic taxa in gross sediments. Further, "The two values defined concentration ranges that were: (1) rarely, (2) occasionally or (3) frequently associated with adverse effects." Comparison of the mean concentrations of heavy metals in mud from the study area with the above ERL and ERM and the three ranges for selected metals listed in Long et al., 1995 (Table 18), indicates that the mean concentrations of As, Cu and Ni in Beaufort Lagoon mud fall into ERL category and Cd, Cr, Pb, Hg and Zn are below ERL. This implies that the concentrations of As, Cu and Ni in the mud of Beaufort Lagoon are above the threshold level where incidences of adverse effects on biota would occasionally occur. However, whether the extrapolation of the guideline suggested by Long et al. (1995) is relevant and applicable to our study in the Beaufort Lagoon is a question that needs to be further investigated. At the outset, to some it would seem that the above comparisons are incompatible, because our metal data is on the mud fraction (<63 μm size) of gross sediments whereas Long et al's guideline is based upon trace metals concentrations in gross sediments which may not be composed entirely of mud. Any infiltration of coarser materials such as gravel or sand size particles can dilute the trace metals in gross sediment. It could be argued that the comparison is invalid because trace metals are almost invariably enriched in the mud fraction compared to gross sediments admixed with the coarses, because of the presence (partitioning) in the mud of chemically more reactive components (e.g., clay minerals and organics). The latter components have high ability to concentrate metals by adsorption and/or formation of organic-clay-metal ligands or complexes. So, in such gross sediments with little mud content the concentrations of metals will likely be low. Although we concede that the above comparison is not totally compatible we, nonetheless, contend that the comparison has some implication on predicting sediment toxicity in the study area. Our contention is based on the general premise that most benthic organisms selectively ingest fine particles (Lee et al., 2000). Therefore, by implication, any high concentration of metal(s) bound to the fine particles would expose the animals to possible adverse effects. It is suggested that any conclusions based on the Long et al.'s guidelines must be substantiated by detailed site-specific cause-effect investigations in Beaufort Lagoon on individual resident organisms. Further, it is to be noted that a lack of consensus exists as to which aspects of the sediment trace metal chemistry are responsible for the adverse effect (Grant and Briggs, 2002). It is suggested that an assessment must be made of the fractions of various metals in the gross sediment that will be potentially available for bio-accumulation. Investigations on the amounts of metals partitioned in various sediment phases [interstitial fluids, extractable phase following acid or acid-reducing agent treatment, acid volatile sulfides (Mucha et al. 2005, and references therein)] will provide more meaningful information on the bioavailability of metals from sediments. The unique problems relating to polar marine toxicology and the future special research needs for the region has been discussed by Chapman and Riddle (2005).

Hydrocarbon Studies

Discussions on the hydrocarbon studies are focused on two aspects; one to elucidate the sources of the hydrocarbons, and the second to assess whether the types and concentrations of hydrocarbons in the Beaufort Lagoon sediments are in any way different than from nearshore sediments elsewhere in the North Slope region.

Criteria to infer hydrocarbon sources

We assessed the relative abundance of the various sources of hydrocarbons (natural oil seep, refined petroleum, fresh crude and natural terrestrial and marine biogenous origin) in each of the sediments analyzed by using, for example, the following guidelines.

Natural crude seepage: Weathered petroleum; Alkane gas chromatogram with a hump (unresolved complex mixture of branched and cyclic components) (Farrington and Tripp, 1977; Simoneit and Kaplan, 1980; Venkatesan et al., 1980).

Fresh petroleum: Unweathered petroleum; characterized by n-alkanes distribution with no odd/even carbon preference throughout the carbon number envelope (Philip, 1985); alkylcyclohexanes and alkylbenzenes are found at significant levels, pristine and phytane are usually more dominant than C_{17} and C_{18} n-alkanes (Zafiriou et al., 1972), triterpenoids are of high thermal maturity characterized by the presence of predominantly 17α-hopanes and moretanes (17$\beta\alpha$-hopanes) (Dastillung and Albrecht, 1976). Alkylated PAHs are more dominant than the parent PAHs (Youngblood and Blumer, 1975).

Biogenic hydrocarbons: Alkane gas chromatogram normally has baseline resolved peaks and does not have a bump (unresolved complex mixture of branched and cyclic components) (Venkatesan and Kaplan, 1982). C_{15}, C_{17} indicates dominant n-alkanes from marine plankton, whereas dominance of C-25 to C-31 n-alkanes indicates terrestrial plant wax, with C-25, 27, 29, 31 and 33 more dominant than the even carbon n-alkanes (resulting in a high odd/even ratio) and with the maximum at C_{29} or

C_{31} n-alkane (Simoneit and Kaplan, 1980; Venkatesan et al., 1980). There was a presence of significant levels of alkanes from marine biota (Blumer et al., 1971). Triterpenoids are of low thermal maturity, characterized by the presence of predominantly 17β-hopanes and hopanes (Dastillung and Albrecht, 1976). There were not many alkylated PAHs.

General characteristics of hydrocarbons as related to their sources

In the following, we enumerate the major criteria that were used to identify the possible sources of hydrocarbons in Beaufort Lagoon sediments.

Alkanes: The alkane gas chromatogram exhibits baseline separation of the components and is generally bimodal with the major maximum at n-C_{27} in 14 of the 20 samples analyzed and at n-C_{29} or n-C_{31} in the remaining sediments (Table 10). Normal alkanes >C_{25} predominate in all the sediment samples with odd/even carbon alkanes ratio in the range from 3.5 to 8.1. These alkanes are derived from higher plants. The secondary maximum at n-C_{17} is characteristic of aquatic algae. The C_{20} and C_{21} olefins found are derived from plankton and bacteria. Although the total n-alkane level varies from 0.1 to 34µg/g similar to the Elson Lagoon sediments, Beaufort Lagoon sediments, in general, seem to exhibit relatively greater vascular inputs than the Elson Lagoon sediments.

In contrast, the O.S. (Oil Seep) sample contains a 100 to 1000-fold concentration of n-alkanes compared to the sediments (i.e., µg/g level vs. ng/g level as found in sediments, Table 10). Very high amounts of n-C_{10} through n-C_{15} and significant levels of alkanes from n-C_{20} to n-C_{32} over a pronounced unresolved hump (UCM = unresolved complex mixture spanning n-C_{21} to n-C_{34}) are found in this sample. The most dominant alkane is n-C_{11}. There is practically no single dominant n-alkane at the high molecular weight end where the odd/even ratio is at 1.3, typical of petroleum input. From the overall profile of the n-alkanes, it appears that the O.S. may be degraded petroleum.

In addition, the L/H ratio ($\sum C_{12}$-C_{19}/$\sum C_{20}$-C_{33} alkanes) of the O.S. is 0.6, which is much higher than in the lagoon sediments (0.05–0.13) as computed from Table 10. Only one sample (BL03-14) has measurable pristane and phytane and the O.S. has neither of the two. The C_{20} and C_{21} planktonic olefins, which are found in all the sediments, are absent in the O.S. sample. Therefore, the *n*-alkanes distribution in the sediment samples is markedly different from that in the O.S. sample, implying that the lagoon sediment is relatively pristine with no measurable petroleum contribution.

Distribution and sources of hydrocarbons in Beaufort Lagoon sediments

Polyaromatic Hydrocarbons (PAHs): The levels of total PAH in the Beaufort Lagoon sediments range from 30 to 710 ng/g (Table 11) and are comparable to sediments from Colville Delta–Prudhoe Bay–Canning Delta (2001), Elson Lagoon (Naidu et al., 2003a) and other nearshore regions of the Beaufort Sea. The PAH composition is dominated by the homologous series of phenanthrenes. The sum of parent PAH and their methyl homologs distribution follows generally in the order: phenanthrenes> naphthalenes≥chrysenes/triphenylenes >fluoranthenes/pyrenes. C_2- naphthalene and C_1-phenanthrene in all the samples and C_1-chrysene in four samples are the most dominant PAH homologs. The general dominance of parent and monomethylated PAHs over higher methylated homologs in the lagoon sediment samples suggests the absence of significant petroleum input in the sediments. Compared to the lower molecular weight PAHs, four and five-ring PAHs are relatively less and perylene is the most dominant parent PAH in all the samples except in BL03-17, which has the least PAH content and contains no perylene. The dominance of perylene in the sediments is consistent with its origin in the Alaskan peats, similar to that found in coastal and other lagoon sediments of north Arctic Alaska (Naidu et al., 2000, 2003a; Macdonald et al., 2004, and references therein). This interpretation is consistent with the relatively light (negative) values of carbon isotope ratios ($\delta^{13}C^o/_{oo}$, Table 1) of all sediments, which point to a predominantly terrestrial (C_3) plant source of OC/organic matter in Beaufort Lagoon (see also Naidu et al., 2000), from peat from coastal erosion (Plate 2).

The O.S. (oil seep) sample contains 208μg/g of total PAHs, about 1000-fold greater than the lagoon sediments, also consistent with the trend in *n*-alkanes content. Unlike in the lagoon sediments, naphthalenes are the most dominant PAHs in the O.S., and, similar to the dominance of low molecular weight C_{10}-C_{15} *n*-alkanes over high molecular weight analogs. Further, the anomalously high value of the naphthalenes/phenanthrenes ratio in the O.S. is observed (7.62) in contrast to the very low range in the sediments (0.03–0.91). C_2-naphthalenes, C_2-phenanthrenes and C_3-chrysenes/triphenylenes are the most dominant methyl homologs, characteristic of petroleum. Neither any PAH beyond C_4-chrysenes/triphenylenes nor perylene are detected in the O.S. The sum of parent PAH and methyl homologs follow the order: naphthalenes>phenanthrenes~ chrysenes/triphenylenes>fluoranthenes/pyrenes.

The overall molecular composition of PAHs in the Beaufort lagoon sediments and a comparison to that of the O.S. sample imply an absence of petroleum in the Beaufort Lagoon sediments, which is consistent with that noted above from the alkanes profiles. The hydrocarbon composition of the sediments from the Beaufort Lagoon is comparable to those from Elson Lagoon and most of the Beaufort Sea sediments investigated by us in previous CMI/MMS studies.

Triterpanoids: Triterpanes are mostly biogenic in the sediments as reflected by the presence of five major components, i.e., 27(17β)-, 29ββ-, 29βα-, 30ββ- hopanes and diploptene (Table 12). The most dominant hopanoid is diploptene and 29ββ-hopane is the second most dominant. Thermally mature 29αβ- and 30αβ-hopanes are present in much smaller/trace amounts relative to biogenic hopanes. Extended hopanes with ≥C_{31} are either not detected or present only in trace quantities and only the R isomer is detected.

Similar to *n*-alkanes, total triterpanes are at the μg/g level and are about 1000-fold greater in the O.S. sample than in the lagoon sediment samples, where they occur at the level of ng/g. Further, the O.S. contains a whole suite of thermally mature αβ-hopanes and none of the biogenic ββ- and βα-hopanes or the hopenes. Both S and R diastereomers of the extended hopanes (i.e., $\geq C_{31}$-hopanes) are present. This hopane's distribution in the O.S. is typical of petroleum/thermally mature sediments.

The trace amounts of isolated, thermally mature (αβ and/or βα-hopanes) biomarkers detected in the sediments most probably derive from peat and/or coal. The overall fingerprint of the triterpanes in sediments of the Beaufort Lagoon does not support any contribution from the O.S.

Steranes: Steranes are generally absent in the Beaufort Lagoon sediment samples. If present, they are only in small/trace amounts, usually about 10 times lower than triterpanes (Table 13). Sediment samples, BL03-12, -13 and -14 contain almost a whole suite of target steranes and at relatively higher levels than the other sediments. This probably implies minimal petroleum input. However, this observation is not supported by triterpane or *n*-alkane profiles. Also, considering the extremely low levels of steranes in these samples, the input from petroleum may not be warranted. The other samples, which contain smaller amounts of a few steranes, are 6B, 18 and 19.

All of the target steranes usually associated with natural weathered oil are present in the O.S. sample and it is about 1000-fold greater than in the lagoon sediments. The steranes profile of O.S. clearly indicates petroleum characteristics.

In summary, normal and cyclic alkanes distribution is characteristic of biogenic origin in all the sediment samples and is different from that of the O.S. sample, thus indicating very little or no petroleum input to the Beaufort Lagoon sediments. The overall profile of alkanes in the Beaufort Lagoon sediments is similar to those of near-shore sediments from the Beaufort Sea that were analyzed by us in previous CMI/MMS projects (Naidu et al., 2001; 2003a). The alkane's distribution of O.S. sample, in contrast, clearly reflects that of petroleum. The overall profiles of the hydrocarbons indicate a significant derivation of them from terrestrial plants, which is corroborated by the OC/N and stable carbon isotope ratios. That the terrestrial organic matter pervades (50%) the organic

matter of sediments throughout the Alaskan–Canadian near-shore is substantiated by more extensive investigations on OC/N, $\delta^{13}C$, $\delta^{15}N$ and *n*-alkanes of sediments of the region (Naidu et al., 2000; Macdonald et al., 2004).

Predicting toxicity in sediments with PAH quality guidelines

As in the case of the trace metals, we have examined the mean concentrations of a group of PAHs in the context of Long et al.'s (1995, 1998) guidelines for identifying hydrocarbon pollution in terms of Effects Range-Low (ERL) and Effects Range-Medium (ERM) (refer to the related discussion above on trace metals). Our study indicates that the mean concentrations of all the PAHs in gross sediments of the Beaufort Lagoon are below the threshold ERL level where incidences of adverse effects would be expected on biota (Table 19).

Conclusions

Interpretations of the trace metal and hydrocarbon data provide the following conclusions. There are no significant disparities in the metal concentrations between the regions exposed to long-term natural oil seep, past anthropogenic activities related to the DEW line military station and the pristine environment of the lagoon. It is suggested that any of the 13 metals investigated that might have been input into the lagoon, from the oil seeps and/or past military activities, are dispersed so widely and diluted that the affect of the point sources on the metal contents are not discernable. Two time-interval comparisons of the mean concentrations of metals in muddy sediments taken at 26-year intervals (1977 to 2003) show a significant decrease in V, an increase in Mn and Cu, and similar values in Cr, Ni and Zn. Data on the rest of the metals were unavailable for 1977. The differences mentioned above likely reflect the differences in granulometry and organic carbon contents between 1977 and 2003 samples. It is to be noted that the 1977 samples were comprised of sandy mud and not entirely of mud as in the case of the 2003 samples. The mean concentrations of all trace metals, except THg, in the mud of Beaufort Lagoon are generally at the same level as those reported by us from the Colville Delta–Prudhoe Bay–Canning Delta region. The significantly higher THg values in

Beaufort Lagoon mud (mean: 57 ng/g) than in the above region (mean: 19 ng/g) is probably due to differences in the natural input of the metal from the hinterland, a proposition that remains to be further investigated. Correlation coefficient analysis between metals, OC and granulometry, suggests that clays and Fe presumably play an important role in metal scavenging and their deposition in Beaufort Lagoon, a conclusion consistent with our results on metal partitioning in the Beaufort Sea near-shore. Based on principal component analysis, it is evident that a southeast-northwest high to low gradient is present in the study area in the concentrations of the trace metals. We attribute this trend to likely net regional variations in granulometry, organic carbon contents and/or possible changes in the natural input of metals contents along the above gradient, rather than a reflection of a gradient resulting from decreasing inputs from potential point sources of contaminants, such as from existing natural oil seeps and/or from the past activities of the Distant Early Warning (DEW) line station located south of Nuvagapak Point.

The hydrocarbon components in gross sediments from the Beaufort Lagoon are biogenic and terrestrial with little petroleum input. Their general composition is very similar to those found in the sediments from Elson Lagoon, Colville Delta–Prudhoe Bay–Canning Delta and the adjacent Canadian deltaic and inner shelf region and the inner shelf of the Beaufort Sea. The data provide no evidence to document the contribution of petroleum hydrocarbons to the Beaufort Lagoon sediments analyzed from the oil seeps located in the vicinity and anthropogenic activities. Petroleum contribution, if there is any to the sediments, is only minimal, below detection levels. The trace metal and hydrocarbon levels are either similar to or below those reported for unpolluted near-shore regions of the world. In summary, the Beaufort Lagoon sediments have remained uncontaminated as far as the analyzed trace metals and hydrocarbons are concerned.

The mean concentrations of As, Cu and Ni in the mud of the Beaufort Lagoon are above the threshold level of Effects Range-Low (ERL) that can cause adverse effects on benthic and demersal organisms. This is a tentative conclusion which must be clarified by further detailed investigations on the metal partitioning patterns and determination of the portions of metals that will likely be made available for possible bioaccumulation.The mean concentrations of all the selected 14 hydrocarbons in the gross sediments of Beaufort Lagoon are below the ERL, which implies that no adverse effects can be expected from hydrocarbons on benthic and demersal organisms.

ACKNOWLEDGEMENTS

This study was funded by the Minerals Management Service, U. S. Department of the Interior through Cooperative Agreement 1435-01-98-CA-30909 (Task Order 74464) between the MMS Alaska OCS Region and the Coastal Marine Institute, University of Alaska Fairbanks. Matching funds were provided by the Institute of Marine Science, University of Alaska Fairbanks and the University of California, Los Angeles. Thanks are due to Zygmunt Kowalik for assistance in the sample collection, and to Franz Mueter for the assistance in the statistical analysis of the trace metal data. The continued encouragement by Vera Alexander, Director, CMI, and the excellent cooperation of Ruth Post and Kathy Carter of CMI, Kate Wedemeyer, Cleve Cowles and R. Prentki of MMS Anchorage throughout this study is appreciated. Grateful thanks are also due to Maggie Billington and Kathy Carter in the preparation of the report.

PUBLICATIONS AND TALKS PRESENTED AT INTERNATIONAL CONFERENCES, CIVIC BODIES AND CMI ANNUAL RESEARCH REVIEW

Naidu, A. S., Kelley, J. J. and Goering, J. J. 2003. Three decades of investigations on heavy metals in coastal sediments, North Arctic Alaska: a synthesis. J. Phys. IV France, 107:913–916.

Kelley, J. J., Naidu, A. S. and Goering, J. J. 2004. Trace metals in sediments of Elson Lagoon (Northwest Arctic Alaska) as related to the Prudhoe Bay industrial region. Talk by Dr. Kelley. Proc. 19th Intn'l. Symposium on Okhotsk Sea and Sea Ice, Mombetsu, Hokkaido, Japan. 175–179.

Naidu, A. S., Kelley, J. J. and Misra, D. 2004. Heavy metal monitoring in sediments of theNorth Alaskan Arctic. Oral presentation (invited) by Dr. Naidu at the Annual Oceania Geosciences Society's (AOGS) First Annual Meeting, Singapore, July 2004. (Abstract Published).

Naidu, A. S., Kelley, J. J., Misra, D. and Venkatesan, M. I. 2003. Trace Metals and Hydrocarbons in Sediments of Beaufort Lagoon, Northeast Arctic Alaska, Exposed to Long-term Natural Oil Seepage, Recent Anthropogenic Activities and Pristine Conditions. Oral presentation by Dr. Naidu at the CMI Annual Research Reviews, February 17, 2004 and March 8, 2005.

Naidu, A. S., Kelley, J. J., Misra, D. and Goering, J. J. 2003. Responsible industrial development in the North Slope nearshore: sediment trace metal history. Luncheon talk given by Dr. Naidu at the Alaska Miner's Association, Fairbanks.

Macdonald, R. W., Naidu, A. S., Yunker, M. B. and Gobeil, C. 2004. The Beaufort Sea: distribution, sources, fluxes and burial of organic carbon. In: R. Stein and R. W. Macdonald (eds.), *The Organic Carbon Cycle in the Arctic Ocean,* Springer-Verlag, Berlin, 177–193.

Misra, D., Naidu, A. S., Kelley, J. J., Venkatesan, M. I. and Mueter, F. 2006. Heavy metals and hydrocarbons in Beaufort Lagoon Sediments, North Arctic Alaska. *In* Y. J. Xu and V. P. Singh (eds.), Coastal Environment and Quality, Vol. II, Chapter 3. ISBN 1-887201-47-5. In press.

Naidu, A. S., Kelley, J. J. and Goering, J. J. 2005. Heavy metals. In: Mark Nuttall (ed.), Encyclopedia of the Arctic, v. 2 (G-N), Routledge, New York, 851–852.

Naidu, A. S., Kelley, J. J. and Misra, D. 2005. Responsible petroleum-related industrial development in the North Slope coastal region, Arctic Alaska: evidence from thirty years of monitoring of trace metals in sediment. Oral presentation by Dr. Naidu at the XII International Conference on Heavy Metals, Rio de Janeiro, Brazil, June 2005. In: Proc. XIII International Conference on Heavy Metals in the Environment, Trindade, R. de B.E., Melamed, R., Sobral, L.G. dos S., and Barbosa, J.P. (Eds.), p. 637–641.

REFERENCES

Bloom, N.S. 1992. On the chemical form of mercury in edible fish and marine invertebrate tissue. Can. J. Aquatic Sci. 49:1010–1017.

Bloom, N.S., G.A. Gill, S. Cappellino, C. Dobbs, L. McShea, C. Driscoll, R. Mason and J. Rudd. 1999. Speciation and cycling of mercury in Lavaca Bay, Texas, sediments. Environ. Sci. Technol. 33(1):7–13. doi: 10.1021/es980379d

Blumer, M., R.R.L. Guillard and T. Chase. 1971. Hydrocarbons of marine phytoplankton. Mar. Biol. 8(3):183–189. doi: 10.1007/BF00355214

Brown, R.E. 1987. Emergency/Survival Handbook, 4th ed. American Outdoor Safety League. Mountaineers Books, Seattle, Washington, 45 p.

Chapman, P.M., and M.J. Riddle. 2005. Polar marine toxicology – future research needs. Mar. Pollut. Bull. 50(9):905–908. doi:10.1016/j.marpolbul.2005.06.001

Crecelius, E.A., J.H. Trefry, M.S. Steinhauer and P.D. Boehm. 1991. Trace metals in sediments from the inner continental shelf of the western Beaufort Sea. Environ. Geol. 18(1):71–79. doi: 10.1007/BF01704579

Currie, D.R., and L.R. Isaacs. 2005. Impact of exploratory offshore drilling on benthic communities in the Minerva gas field, Port Campbell, Australia. Mar. Environ. Res. 59(3):217–233. doi:10.1016/j.marenvres.2004.05.001

Dastillung, M., and P. Albrecht. 1976. Molecular test for oil pollution in surface sediments. Mar. Pollut. Bull. 7(1):13–15. doi:10.1016/0025-326X(76)90282-4

Douglas, D.C., P.E. Reynolds and E.B. Rhode [eds.]. 2002. Arctic Refuge Coastal Plain Terrestrial Wildlife Research Summaries. Biological Science Report, USGS/BRD/BSR-2002-0001, U.S. Geol. Survey, Reston, Virginia, 75 p.

Farrington, J.W., and B.W. Tripp. 1977. Hydrocarbons in western North Atlantic surface sediments. Geochim. Cosmochim. Acta 41(11):1627–1641. doi:10.1016/0016-7037(77)90173-9

Folk, R. 1968. Petrology of Sedimentary Rocks. Hemphill Publishing Co., Austin, Texas, 70 p.

Grant, A., and A.D. Briggs 2002. Toxicity of sediments from around a North Sea oil platform: Are metals or hydrocarbons responsible for ecological impacts? Mar. Environ. Res. 53(1):95–116. doi:10.1016/S0141-1136(01)00114-3

Krantzberg, G., J.H. Hartig and M.A. Zarull. 2000. Sediment management: Deciding when to intervene. Environ. Sci. Technol. 34(1):22A–27A.

Lee, B.-G., S.B. Griscom, J.-S. Lee, H.J. Choi, C.-H. Koh, S.N. Luoma and N.S. Fisher. 2000. Influences of dietary uptake and reactive sulfides on metal bioavailability from aquatic sediments. Science 287(5451):282–284. doi: 10.1126/science.287.5451.282

Lee, H.J., and P.L. Wiberg. 2002. Character, fate, and biological effects of contaminated, effluent-affected sediment on the Palos Verdes margin, southern California: An overview. Cont. Shelf Res. 22(6–7):835–840. doi:10.1016/S0278-4343(01)00106-6

Long, E.R., L.J. Field and D.D. MacDonald. 1998. Predicting toxicity in marine sediments with numerical sediment quality guidelines. Environ. Toxicol. Chem. 17(4):714–727. doi: 10.1897/1551-5028(1998)017<0714:PTIMSW>2.3.CO;2

Long, E R., D.D. MacDonald, S.L. Smith and F.D. Calder. 1995. Incidence of adverse biological effects within ranges of chemical concentrations in marine and estuarine sediments. Environ. Manage. 19:81–97.

Macdonald, R.W. 1982. An examination of metal inputs to the Southern Beaufort Sea by disposal of waste barite in drilling fluid. Ocean Manage. 8(1):29–49. doi:10.1016/0302-184X(82)90012-9

Macdonald, R.W., A.S. Naidu, M.B. Yunker and C. Gobeil. 2004. The Beaufort Sea: Distribution, sources, fluxes, and burial rates of organic carbon, p. 177–192. *In* R. Stein and R.W. Macdonald [eds.], The Organic Carbon Cycle in the Arctic Ocean. Springer, Berlin/New York.

Mucha, A.P., M. Teresa, S.D. Vasconcelos and A.A. Bordalo. 2005. Spatial and seasonal variations of the macrobenthic community and metal contamination in the Douro estuary (Portugal). Mar. Environ. Res. 60(5):531–550. doi:10.1016/j.marenvres.2004.12.004

Naidu, A.S. 1981. Sources, Transport Pathways, Depositional Sites and Dynamics of Sediments in the Lagoon and Adjacent Shallow Marine Region, Northern Arctic Alaska. Annual Report to NOAA–OCSEAP Office, Boulder, Colorado, 39 p.

Naidu, A.S. 1985. Organic carbon, nitrogen, and C/N ratios of deltaic sediments, North Arctic Alaska, p. 311–321. *In* SCOPE/UNEP Sonderband Heft 58, Mitt. Geol-Paläont. Inst., Univ. Hamburg, Germany.

Naidu, A.S., L.W. Cooper, B.P. Finney, R.W. Macdonald, C. Alexander and I.P. Semiletov. 2000. Organic carbon isotope ratios (δ^{13}C) of Arctic Amerasian continental shelf sediments, p. 522–532. *In* R. Stein [ed.], Circum-Arctic River Discharge and Its Geological Record, Int. J. Earth Sci., Spec. Issue, Vol. 89.

Naidu, A.S., J.J. Goering, J.J. Kelley and M.I. Venkatesan. 2001. Historical Changes in Trace Metals and Hydrocarbons in the Inner Shelf, Beaufort Sea: Prior and Subsequent to Petroleum-Related Industrial Developments. Final Report. OCS Study MMS 2001-061, University of Alaska Coastal Marine Institute, University of Alaska Fairbanks and USDOI, MMS, Alaska OCS Region, 80 p.

Naidu, A.S., J.J. Kelley and J.J. Goering. 2003a. Three decades of investigations on heavy metals in coastal sediments, North Arctic Alaska: A synthesis. J. Phys. IV France 107:913–916.

Naidu, A.S., J.J. Kelley, J.J. Goering and M.I. Venkatesan. 2003b. Trace Metals and Hydrocarbons in Sediments of Elson Lagoon (Barrow, Northwest Arctic Alaska) as Related to the Prudhoe Bay Industrial Region. Final Report. OCS Study MMS 2003-057, University of Alaska Coastal Marine Institute, University of Alaska Fairbanks and USDOI, MMS, Alaska OCS Region, 33 p.

Neff, J.M. 2002. Fates and effects of mercury from oil and gas exploration and production operations in the marine environment. Battelle Memorial Institute. Report prepared for the American Petroleum Institute, Washington, D.C., 136 p.

NORTECH (Northern Technical Services). 1981. Beaufort Sea Drilling Effluent Disposal Study. Report for SOHIO Alaska Petroleum Co., Anchorage, 329 p.

Philp, R.P. 1985. Fossil Fuel Biomarkers: Applications and Spectra. Methods in Geochemistry and Geophysics, 23. Elsevier, New York, 294 p.

Simoneit, B.R.T., and I.R. Kaplan. 1980. Triterpenoids as molecular indicators of paleoseepage in recent sediments of the Southern California Bight. Mar. Environ. Res. 3(2):113–128. doi:10.1016/0141-1136(80)90020-3

Snyder-Conn, E., D. Densmore, C. Moitoret and J. Stroebele. 1990. Persistence of trace metals in shallow arctic marine sediments contaminated by drilling effluents. Oil & Chem. Pollut. 7(3):225–247. doi:10.1016/S0269-8579(05)80028-0

Steinhauer, M.S., and P.D. Boehm. 1992. The composition and distribution of saturated and aromatic hydrocarbons in nearshore sediments, river sediments, and coastal peat of the Alaskan Beaufort Sea: Implications for detecting anthropogenic hydrocarbon inputs. Mar. Environ. Res. 33(4):223–253. doi:10.1016/0141-1136(92)90140-H

Sweeney, M.D. 1984. Heavy Metals in the Sediments of an Arctic Lagoon, Northern Alaska. M.S. Thesis, Univ. Alaska Fairbanks, 256 p.

Sweeney, M.D., and A.S. Naidu. 1989. Heavy metals in the sediments of the inner shelf of the Beaufort Sea, northern arctic Alaska. Mar. Pollut. Bull. 20(3):140–143. doi:10.1016/0025-326X(88)90820-X

Thompson, B., B. Anderson, J. Hunt, K. Taberski and B. Phillips. 1999. Relationships between sediment contamination and toxicity in San Francisco Bay. Mar. Environ. Res. 48(4–5):285–309. doi:10.1016/S0141-1136(99)00060-4

Trefry, J.H., R.D. Rember, R.P. Trocine and J.S. Brown. 2003. Trace metals in sediments near offshore oil exploration and production sites in the Alaskan Arctic. Environmental Geol. 45(2):149–160. doi: 10.1007/s00254-003-0882-2

USGS (U.S. Geological Survey) ANWR Assessment Team. 1999. The Oil and Gas Resource Potential of the Arctic National Wildlife Refuge 1002 Area, Alaska. U.S. Geolological Survey Open File Report 98–34. http://energy.cr.usgs.gov/OF98-34

Valette-Silver, N. [ed.] 1999. Using sediments and biota to assess coastal and estuarine contamination. Mar. Environ. Res., Spec. Issue, Vol. 48(4–5), 494 p.

Venkatesan, M.I. 1994. Historical Trends in the Deposition of Organic Pollutants in the Southern California Bight. UCLA, Final report to NOAA, 35 p.

Venkatesan, M.I., S. Brenner, E. Ruth, J. Bonilla and I.R. Kaplan. 1980. Hydrocarbons in age-dated sediment cores from two basins in the Southern California Bight. Geochim. Cosmochim. Acta 44(6):789–802. doi:10.1016/0016-7037(80)90260-4

Venkatesan, M.I., and I.R. Kaplan. 1982. Distribution and transport of hydrocarbons in surface sediments of the Alaskan outer continental shelf. Geochim. Cosmochim. Acta 46(11):2135–2149. doi:10.1016/0016-7037(82)90190-9

Venkatesan, M.I., E. Ruth, S. Steinberg and I.R. Kaplan. 1987. Organic geochemistry of sediments from the continental margin off southern New England, U.S.A. – Part II. Lipids. Mar. Chem. 21(3):267–299. doi:10.1016/0304-4203(87)90063-6

Weis, J.S., J. Skurnick and P. Weis. 2004. Studies of a contaminated brackish marsh in the Hackensack Meadowlands of Northeastern New Jersey: Benthic communities and metal contamination. Mar. Pollut. Bull. 49(11–12):1025–1035. doi:10.1016/j.marpolbul.2004.07.006

Youngblood, W.W., and M. Blumer. 1975. Polycyclic aromatic hydrocarbons in the environment: Homologous series in soils and recent marine sediments. Geochim. Cosmochim. Acta 39(9):1303–1314. doi:10.1016/0016-7037(75)90137-4

Zafiriou, O.C., M. Blumer and J. Myers. 1972. Correlation of oils and oil products by gas chromatography. Woods Hole Oceanographic Institution Tech. Rep. 72–55, 110 p

EXECUTIVE SUMMARY

This project addressed the concern that concentrations of trace metals and hydrocarbons in the sediments of the Alaskan Arctic can occur as a result of petroleum exploration and production activities. Lagoon sediments of the North Slope, if they were to be the ultimate sink for both organic and inorganic anthropogenic chemicals, could be a major source of contaminants for benthic animals as well as organisms which have a close link with sediments and which serve as transfer pathways of contaminants to higher trophic levels. Recognizing the pending lease sales scheduled by MMS in 2003–2007 we have extended our investigations to establish baselines on trace metals and hydrocarbons in the sediments of the Beaufort Lagoon located at the remote eastern margin of the north Alaskan Arctic coast and far from intense industrial activities.

This report presents the highlights of a two-year study (2003–2005) which has as its major objective the measurement of the concentrations of a suite of 12 trace metals (copper (Cu), chromium (Cr), cadmium (Cd), nickel (Ni), vanadium (V), lead (Pb), tin (Sn), zinc (Zn), arsenis (As), barium (Ba), iron (Fe) and manganese (Mn) in the mud fraction (<63 um size), and total mercury (THg), sediment grain size, organic carbon (OC) and hydrocarbons (normal and isoprenoid alkanes, triterpenoids and steranes and polycyclic aromatic hydrocarbons) in the gross sediments of the Beaufort Lagoon. The choice of the above metals and hydrocarbons is based on the fact that these chemicals are often present in drilling effluents, crude, and petroleum development and production activities. The purpose of this study was to close a gap in the baselines for sediment metals and hydrocarbons for a remote region of the North Slope Coast.

Sediment samples (Van Veen grab) from the Beaufort Lagoon were collected at 22 selected stations spread over three sectors. Six of the samples were in close proximity to natural oil seeps, another six samples from an area that was impacted by military activities connected with a DEW line station (now defunct), and a third suite of 10 samples from east lagoon which is presumed pristine. The methods for the analyses of the trace metals and hydrocarbons on the sediments was essentially the same as those adopted in previously supported CMI/MMS studies elsewhere along the North Slope nearshore region. The QA/QC (quality assurance/quality control) protocol prescribed by the U.S. Environmental Protection Agency (EPA) for metal analysis was followed. QA/QC for the organic analyses included successful participation in the (NOAA/National Status and Trends Program).

Statistical analysis consisted of the determination of the correlation coefficients between trace metals, OC, N, and the silt and clay percents in the mud fraction to deduce the geochemical partitioning of the metals in the mud analyzed. Cluster analysis was conducted to determine if there were groupings of samples based on trace metal concentrations. In addition, principal component analysis was conducted to deduce the cause of the regional variations in metal concentrations.

Interpretations of the trace metal and hydrocarbon data provide the following conclusions. There are no significant disparities in the metal concentrations between the regions exposed to long-term natural oil seep, past anthropogenic activities related to the DEW line military station and the pristine environment of the lagoon. Any of the trace metals investigated in this study that might have originated from oil seeps or human activity are widely dispersed and diluted. The effect of any point sources on the metal content in the sediment is not discernable.

Two time interval comparisons of the mean concentrations of metals in muddy sediments taken at 26-year intervals (1977–2003) show a significant decrease in V, an increase in Mn and Cu, and similar values in Cr, Ni and Zn. These differences likely reflect the differences in granulometry and organic carbon contents between the 1977 and 2003 samples.

The mean concentration of all trace metals in the mud of Beaufort Lagoon are generally at the same level as those reported by us from the

Colville Delta, Prudhoe Bay-Canning Delta region.

The significantly higher Hg values in Beaufort Lagoon gross sediments (mean: 57ng/g) than in the Colville Delta-Prudhoe Bay-Canning Delta region (mean: 19 ng/g) are probably due to differences in the natural input of the metal from the hinterland, a proposition that remains to be further investigated.

Correlation coefficient analysis between metals, OC, and granulometry, suggests that clays and Fe oxy-hydroxide presumably play an important role in metal scavenging and their deposition in the Beaufort Lagoon. This conclusion is consistent with our results on metal partitioning in the adjacent nearshore regions of Beaufort Sea.

Based on principal component analysis, it is evident that a southeast-northwest high to low gradient is present in the study area in the concentrations of the trace metals. This trend may be attributed to net regional variations in granulometry, organic carbon contents and/or possible changes in the natural input of metals contents along the above gradients, rather than a reflection of a gradient resulting from decreasing inputs from potential point sources of contaminants, such as from natural oil seeps and/or from past activities of the Distant Early

Warning (DEW) line station located south of Nuvagapak Point.

The hydrocarbon components in gross sediments from the Beaufort Lagoon are biogenic and terrestrial. Their general composition is very similar to those found in the sediments from Elson Lagoon, Colville Delta, Prudhoe Bay, Canning Delta and adjacent Canadian deltaic and inner shelf region and the inner shelf of the Beaufort Sea. The data provide no evidence to document the contribution of petroleum hydrocarbons to the Beaufort Lagoon sediments analyzed from the oil seeps located in the vicinity and anthropogenic activities. The trace metal and hydrocarbon levels are either similar to or below those reported for unpolluted near-shore regions of the world. The Beaufort Lagoon sediments have remained uncontaminated as far as the analyzed trace metals and hydrocarbons are concerned.

The mean concentrations of As, Cu and Ni in the mud of the Beaufort Lagoon are above the threshold level of the Effects Range-low (ERL), as stated in Long et al., (1995, 1998), that can cause adverse effects on benthic and demersal organisms. However, the mean concentrations of all the selected 14 hydrocarbons in the gross sediments of Beaufort Lagoon are below the ERL, which implies that no adverse effects can be expected from current levels of hydrocarbons on the above organisms.

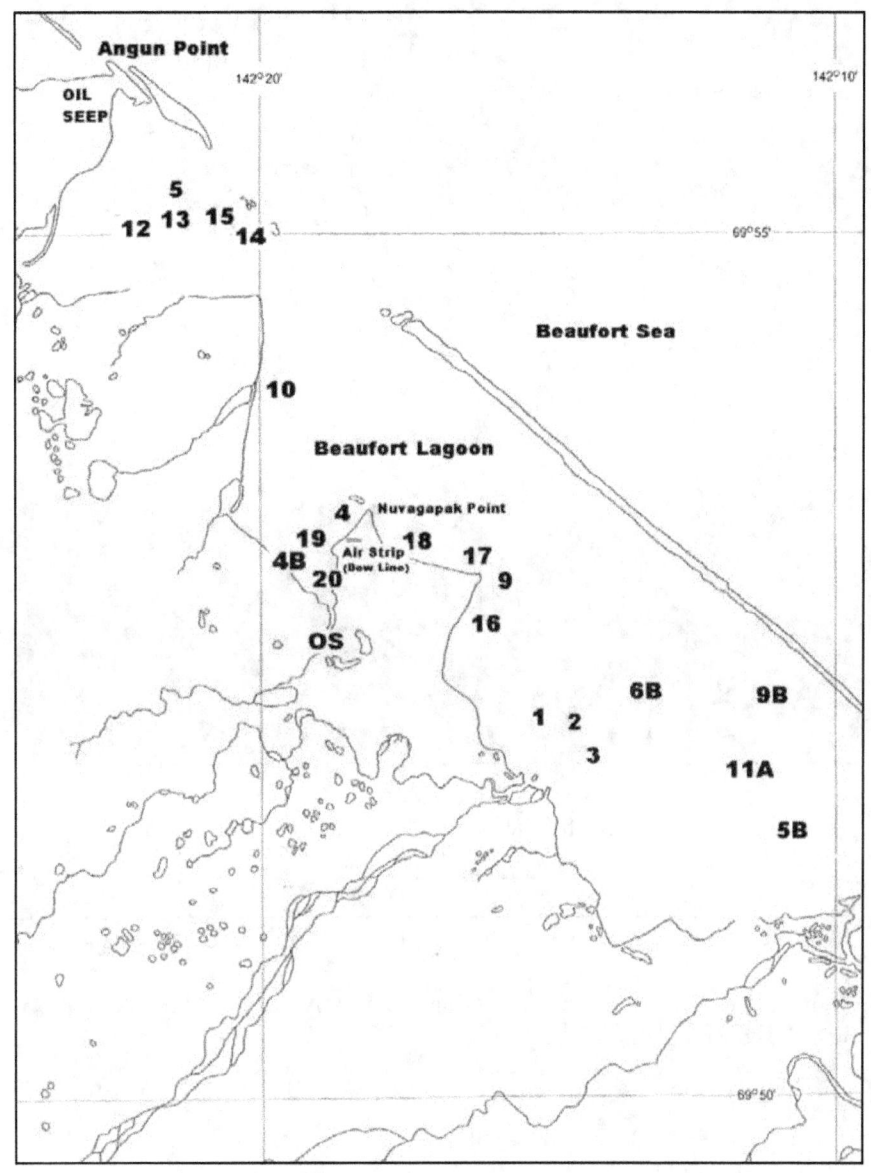

Figure 1: Study area showing locations of sediment samples in the Beaufort Lagoon.

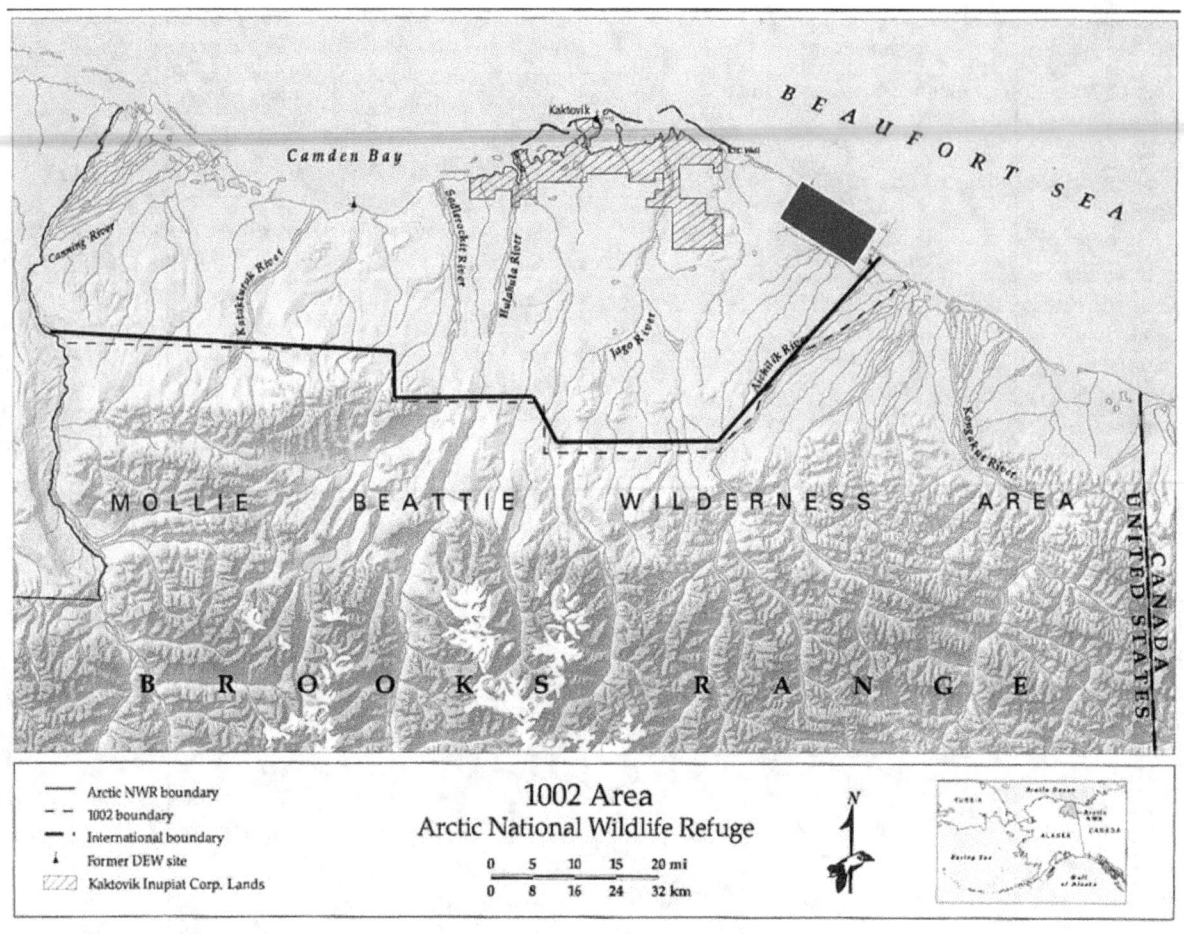

Figure 2: Map showing the study area (in filled rectangle) relative to the Arctic National Wildlife Refuge (ANWR) including the coastal plain unit.

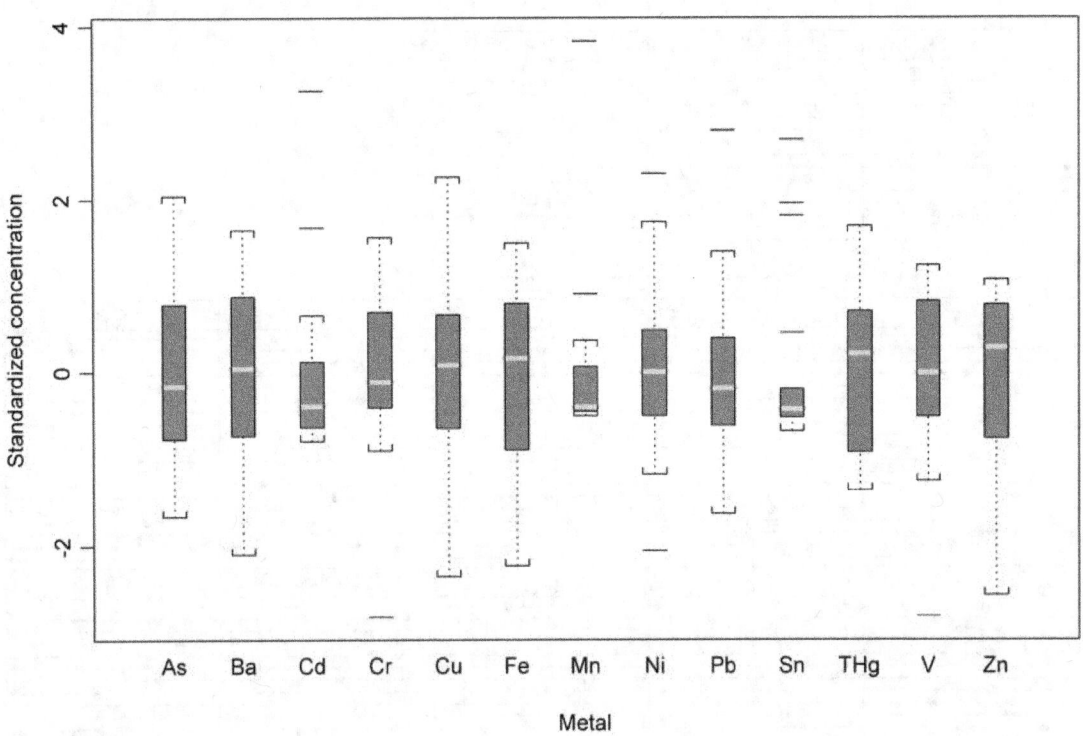

Figure 3: Boxplots of standardized concentrations of 12 metals in Beaufort Lagoon sediments.

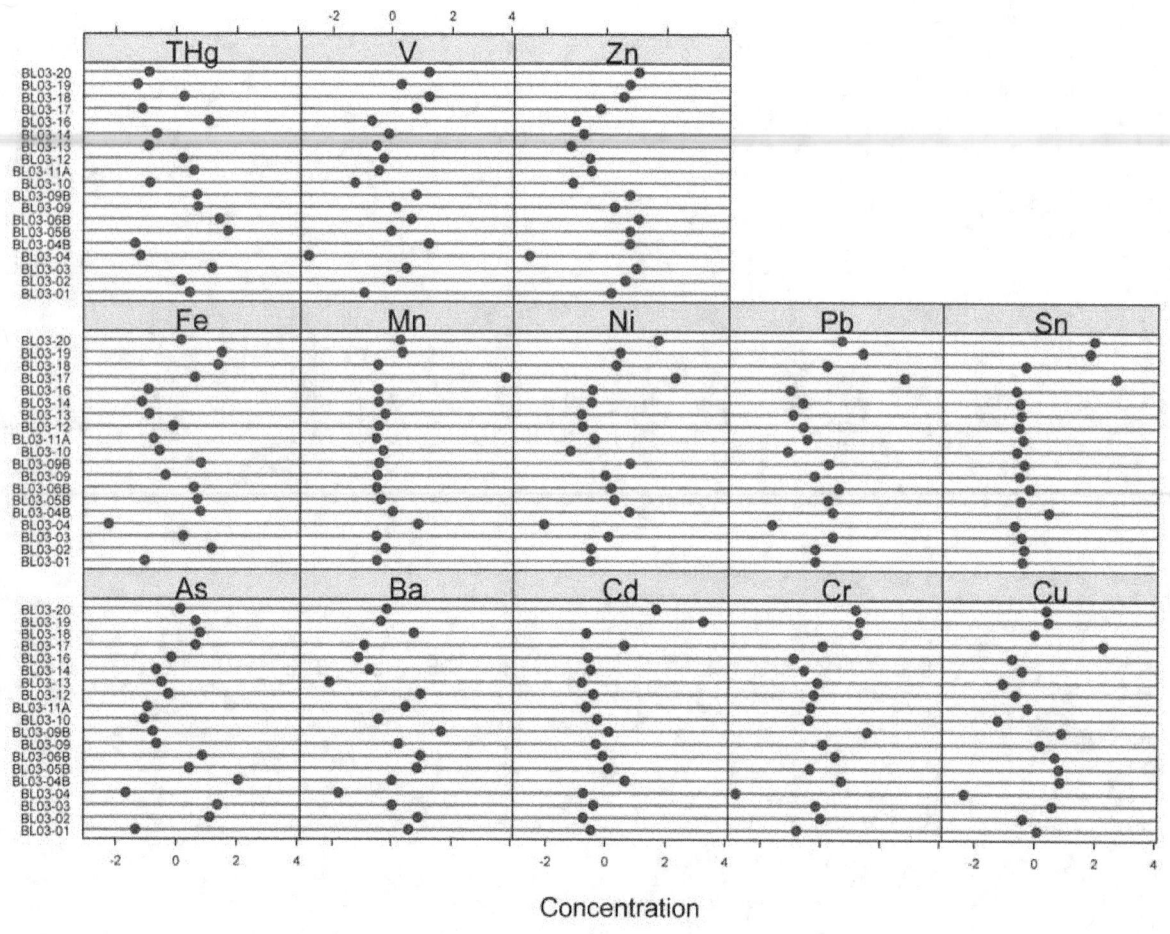

Figure 4: Dotplots of metal concentrations for 12 metals by station in Beaufort Lagoon.

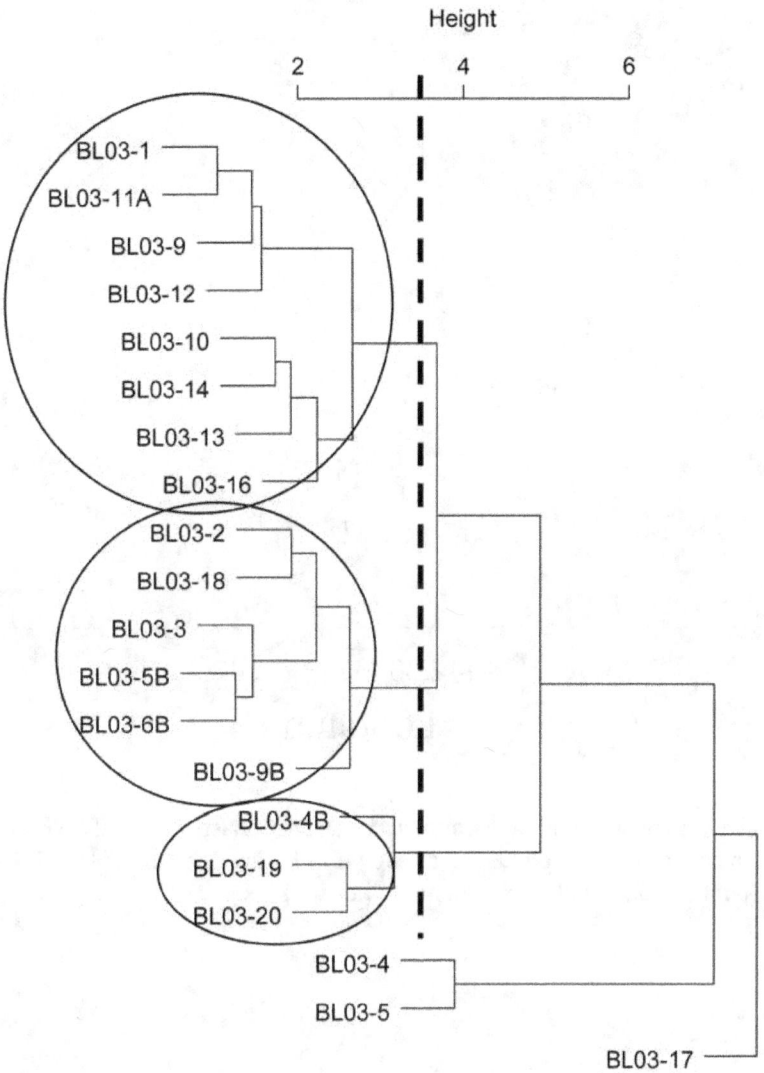

Figure 5: Dendrogram showing Ward's linkage clustering (Euclidean distances) based on concentrations of 12 metals measured at each station.

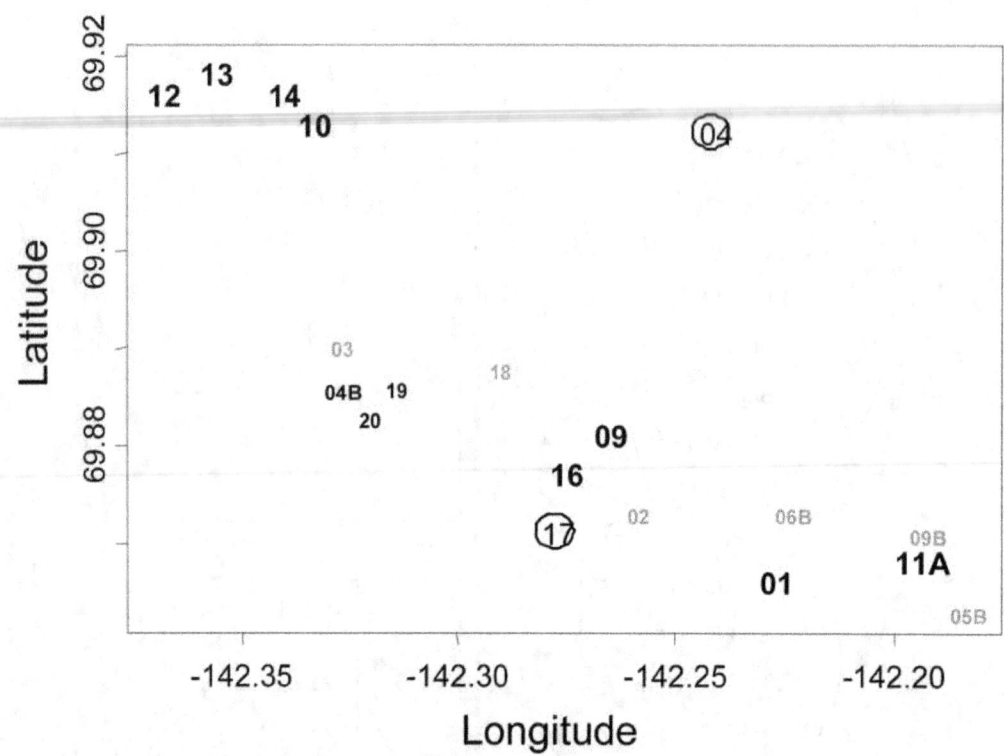

Figure 6: Map showing relative locations of stations (coastline not shown) and group membership corresponding to clusters as shown in Figure 5. Stations BL03-4 and BL03-17 (circled) did not cluster with any other stations.

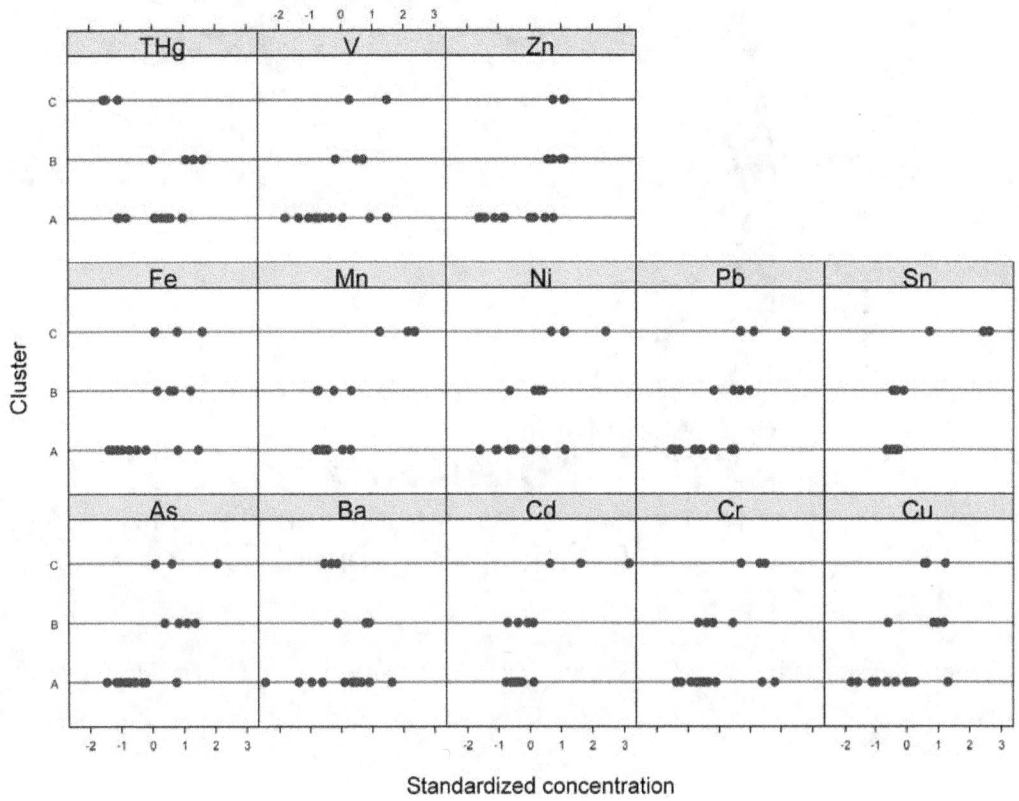

Figure 7: Dotplots of metal concentrations for 12 metals by cluster (see Fig. 5 for clusters).

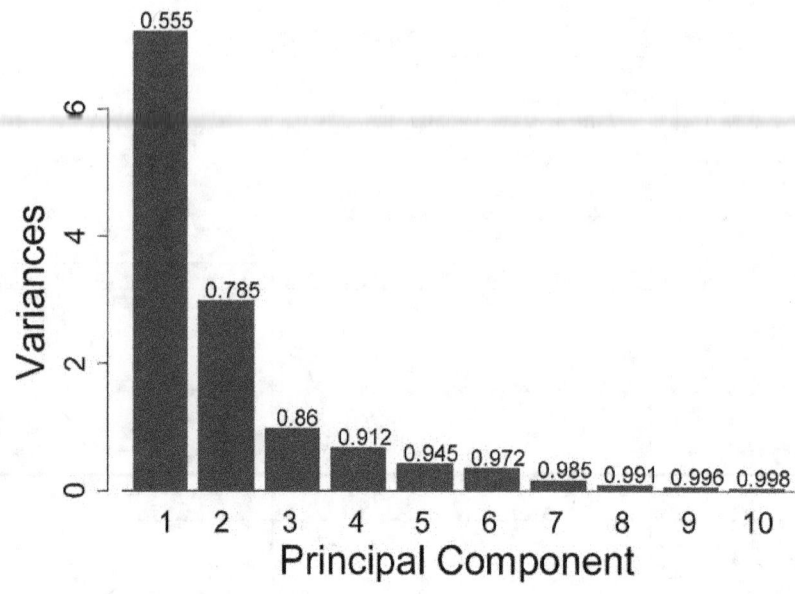

Figure 8: Cumulative amount of variance explained by the first ten Principal Components.

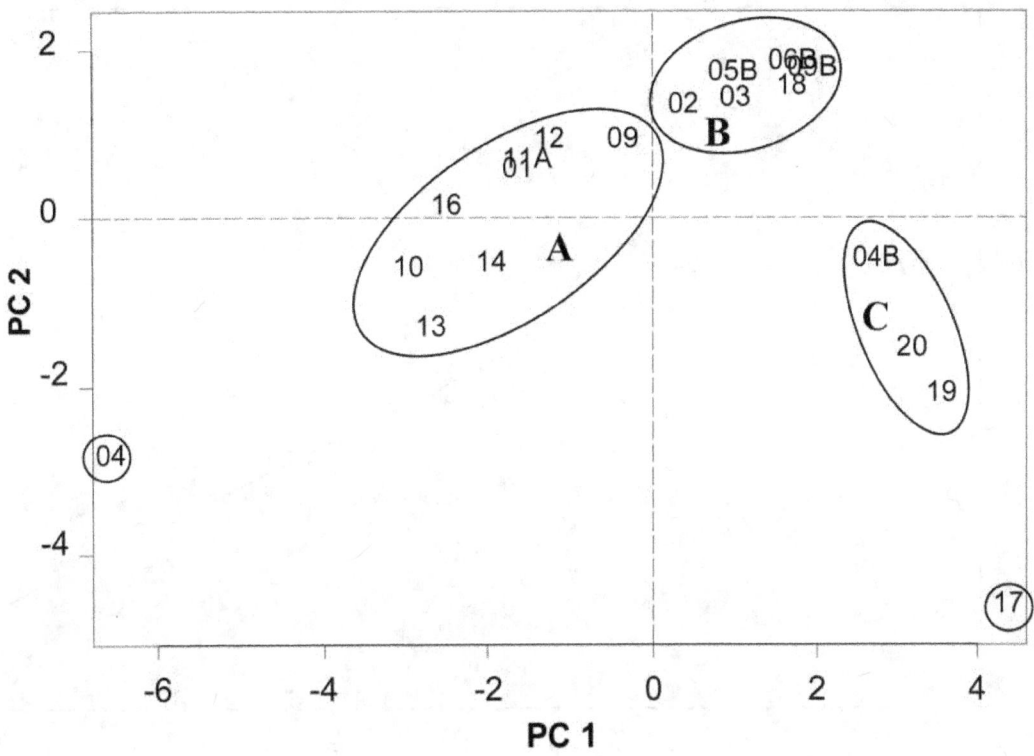

Figure 9: Beaufort Lagoon stations in the space of the first two principal components. Groups identified by a cluster analysis (see Fig. 5) are indicated.

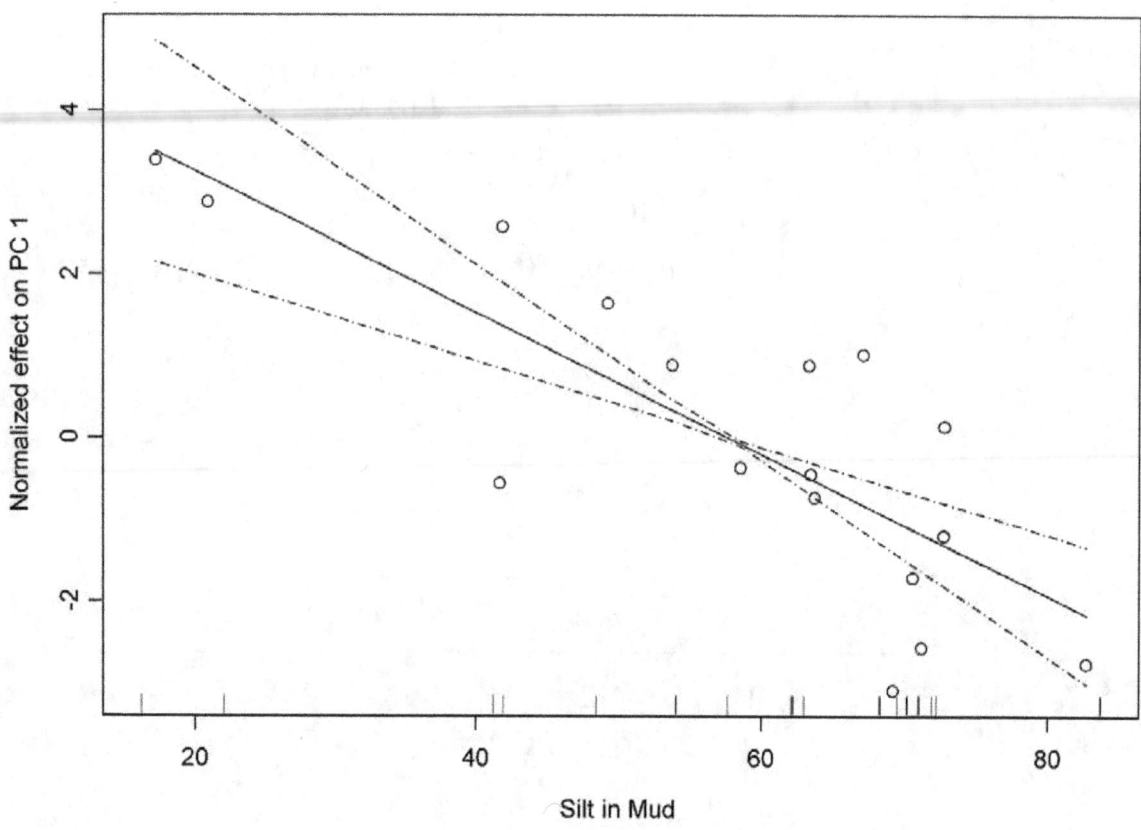

Figure 10: Partial fit of PC 1 on silt in mud fraction after accounting for effects of latitude (stations BL03-4 and BL03-17 were excluded from regression).

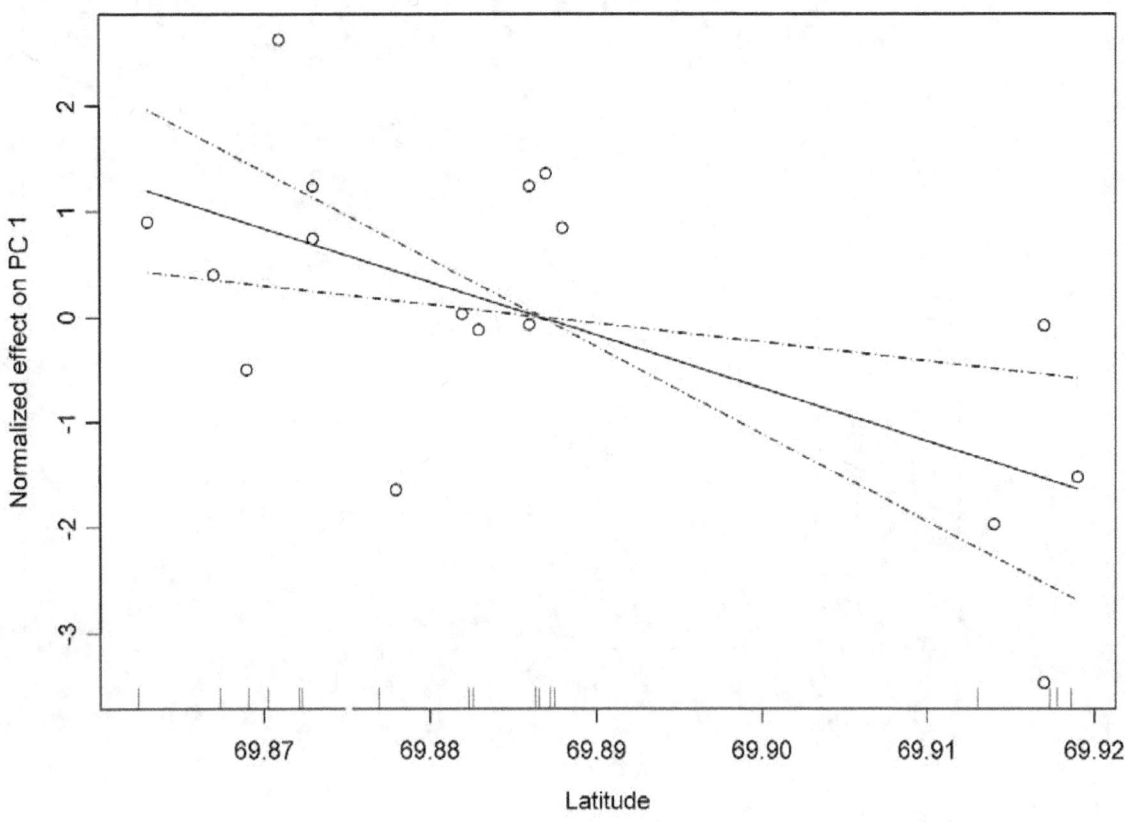

Figure 11: Partial fit of PC 1 on latitude after accounting for effects of silt in mud fraction (stations BL03-4 and BL03-17 were excluded from regression).

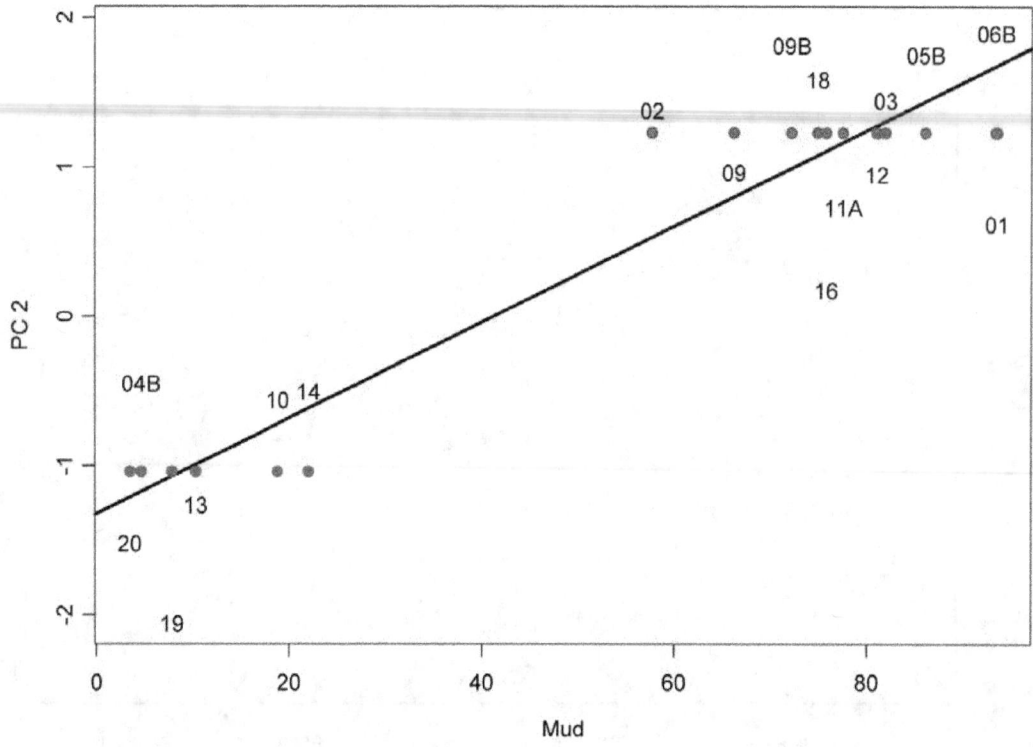

Figure 12: Linear regression of PC 2 on percentage of mud in sediment (stations BL03-4 and BL03-17 were excluded from regression). Red points show mean values of PC 2 corresponding to mud concentrations below and above 50%.

Table 1: Sample locations, grain sizes, organic carbon (OC), nitrogen (N), OC/N, and stable isotopes of OC (δ^{13}C ‰) and N (δ^{15}N) of Beaufort Lagoon sediments.

Sample	Lat °N	Long °W	Solids %	Gravel %	Sand %	Silt %	Clay %	Mud %	OC %	N %	OC/N	δ^{13}C	δ^{15}N
BL03-1	69.87	142.23	53.4	0.00	6.43	77.39	16.18	93.57	2.39	0.22	10.86	-26.94	1.88
BL03-2	69.87	142.26	67.9	0.00	42.28	36.63	21.09	57.72	2.33	0.20	11.60	-26.89	2.02
BL03-3	69.89	142.33	51.9	0.00	18.11	51.87	30.02	81.89	2.17	0.20	10.85	-26.36	0.83
BL03-4	69.91	142.24	79.5	0.00	95.55	0.09	4.36	4.45	1.72	0.17	10.11	-24.98	2.90
BL03-4B	69.89	142.33	91.5	92.87	2.54	1.92	2.66	4.59	3.29	0.32	10.28	-26.99	3.09
BL03-5	69.93	142.36	99.10	NA	NA	NA	NA	NA	NA	NA	NA	NA	NA
BL03-5B	69.86	142.18	52.9	0.00	13.94	50.36	35.70	86.06	2.00	0.18	11.11	-26.24	1.60
BL03-6B	69.87	142.22	56.8	0.00	6.56	50.22	43.22	93.44	2.02	0.19	10.63	-26.49	2.05
BL03-9	69.88	142.27	61.2	0.28	33.60	42.13	23.98	66.12	3.96	0.36	11.00	-27.35	1.95
BL03-9B	69.87	142.19	65.0	0.00	27.86	48.44	23.69	72.14	2.27	0.19	11.94	-26.24	1.79
BL03-10	69.91	142.33	74.9	0.00	81.25	13.24	5.50	18.75	2.38	0.20	11.90	-27.14	3.41
BL03-11A	69.87	142.20	61.9	0.00	22.51	55.19	22.30	77.49	1.55	0.13	11.92	-27.26	1.07
BL03-12	69.92	142.37	61.4	0.00	19.01	58.97	22.02	80.99	2.04	0.17	12.00	-26.85	2.21
BL03-13	69.92	142.36	76.6	0.00	89.76	7.45	2.79	10.24	1.43	0.12	11.91	-26.85	2.07
BL03-14	69.92	142.34	67.0	0.00	77.97	9.18	12.85	22.03	1.66	0.15	11.07	-26.96	1.75
BL03-15	69.92	142.34	NA	0.00	83.42	3.15	13.42	16.58	1.76	0.17	10.35	-26.49	1.76
BL03-16	69.88	142.28	43.8	0.00	24.24	52.46	23.30	75.76	3.20	0.26	12.30	-27.53	1.80
BL03-17	69.87	142.28	79.6	0.12	97.88	0.05	1.95	1.99	2.57	0.30	8.56	-25.84	3.12
BL03-18	69.89	142.29	56.4	0.00	25.17	36.81	38.02	74.83	2.60	0.23	11.30	-26.85	2.83
BL03-19	69.89	142.31	89.8	28.60	63.62	1.34	6.45	7.78	4.05	0.38	10.66	-26.76	1.80
BL03-20	69.88	142.32	79.3	37.75	58.80	0.72	2.73	3.45	3.75	0.37	10.13	-27.21	2.23
OS	69.88	142.31	NA	NA	NA	NA	NA	NA	NA	NA	NA	NA	NA

Table 2: Concentrations of metals in Beaufort Lagoon sediments. All are µg/g, except Hg (ng/g) and Fe (%).

Sample	V µg/g	Cr	Mn	Ni	Cu	Zn	As	Cd	Sn	Ba	Pb µg/g	THg ng/g	Fe %
BL03-1	110	68.6	318	36.9	38.5	98.4	10.9	0.224	1.78	559	16.8	68.5	2.64
BL03-2	121	73.7	506	37.0	34.9	105	17.7	0.195	1.83	585	16.8	58.8	3.44
BL03-3	127	72.7	311	40.6	42.3	110	18.4	0.233	1.76	512	19.1	94.6	3.10
BL03-4	87.3	55.5	1222	27.2	19.9	60.2	10.0	0.196	1.53	355	11.0	11.7	2.21
BL03-4B	136	78.2	668	44.9	44.3	107	20.3	0.345	2.65	511	19.1	5.2	3.31
BL03-5	94.7	59.9	182	25.7	16.2	48.2	6.9	0.085	1.32	436	12.0	118	2.17
BL03-5B	121	71.4	407	41.8	44.0	107	15.8	0.286	1.73	583	18.5	113	3.27
BL03-6B	129	76.9	319	41.2	43.0	111	17.0	0.266	2.01	592	19.9	103	3.23
BL03-9	123	74.2	339	40.0	39.2	100	12.8	0.242	1.69	530	16.7	78.1	2.89
BL03-9B	131	83.8	370	45.0	44.7	107	12.5	0.287	1.83	649	18.6	77.1	3.31
BL03-10	106	71.1	457	32.7	28.5	80.4	11.7	0.246	1.60	473	13.1	22.8	2.82
BL03-11A	116	71.5	305	37.7	36.1	89.1	12.0	0.206	1.80	550	15.7	73.4	2.75
BL03-12	118	72.2	364	35.2	33.0	88.5	13.9	0.232	1.68	592	15.2	60.6	2.98
BL03-13	115	73.0	503	35.0	29.7	79.5	13.3	0.190	1.74	329	13.8	20.9	2.69
BL03-14	120	70.2	359	37.1	34.6	85.5	12.8	0.223	1.71	446	15.1	30.1	2.61
BL03-16	113	67.9	351	37.3	32.1	81.9	14.2	0.214	1.58	413	13.4	90.7	2.69
BL03-17	131	74.1	3132	54.3	55.2	93.3	16.4	0.341	4.86	430	28.7	13.4	3.24
BL03-18	136	81.7	346	42.2	37.9	104	16.8	0.207	1.88	572	18.3	62.0	3.52
BL03-19	125	82.2	868	43.0	41.2	107	16.4	0.623	3.99	479	23.1	7.89	3.56
BL03-20	136	81.3	829	50.8	40.8	111	15.0	0.454	4.13	496	20.3	21.5	3.07
A-Mean	120	73.0	608	39.0	37.0	94	14.0	0.265	2.00	505	17.0	57.0	2.98
Std AM	13	7.0	643	6.8	8.9	17	3.2	0.110	0.98	85	4.1	37.3	0.4004
G-Mean	119	73.0	472	39.0	36.0	92	14.0	0.246	2.00	497	17.0	41.0	2.95
Std GM	13	7.0	658	6.9	9.0	17	3.2	0.110	0.99	85	4.1	40.7	0.4014
% CV	11	9.7	139	17.7	25.2	19	23.2	46.400	49.40	17	24.3	99.9	14

A-Mean: Arithmetic mean
Std AM: Standard deviation of arithmetic mean
G-Mean: Geometric mean
Std GM: Standard deviation of geometric mean
% CV: Percent coefficient of variation

Table 3: Results of the QA/QC analysis concerning calibration verification.

Analyte (unit)	Batch ID	ICV-TV	ICV-Obs	ICV-Rec	CCV1-TV	CCV1-Obs	CCV1-Rec	CCV2-TV	CCV2-Obs	CCV2-Rec
V (µg/L)	A	50	45.3523091	90.7046182	10	10.10702359	101.0702359	10	9.869872351	98.69872351
Cr	A	50	46.96249819	93.92499637	10	10.42038436	104.2038436	10	10.31545133	103.1545133
Mn	A	50	45.61942801	91.23885601	10	10.47879367	104.7879367	10	10.295745	102.695745
Fe	A	100	73.05313706	73.05313706	50.00000381	39.06361265	78.12721935	50.00000381	38.63918732	77.27836875
Ni	A	50	50.8867821	101.7735642	10	10.68007653	106.8007653	10	10.66856767	106.6856767
Cu	A	50	50.30532361	100.6106472	10	10.60041579	106.0041579	10	10.43874602	104.3874602
Zn	A	50	51.36481686	102.7296337	20	20.94026515	104.7013258	20	20.4971425	102.485713
As	A	50	45.45553065	90.91106131	10	10.3048842	103.048842	10	10.02663014	100.2663014
Cd	A	5	4.649514064	92.99028129	1	1.029401306	102.9401306	1	1.003388809	100.3388809
Sn	A	50	53.76962124	107.5392425		2.003951832			1.911100463	
Ba	A	100	97.20926536	97.20926536	10	9.892735523	98.92735523	10	9.796689174	97.96689174
Pb (µg/L)	A	5	5.148574426	102.9714885	2	2.219005835	110.9502917	2	2.193173488	109.6686744
THg (ng/L)	B	15	15.14149028	100.9432685	20	19.85846544	99.29232721	20	20.06355132	100.3177566

Analyte (unit)	Batch ID	CCV3-TV	CCV3-Obs	CCV3-Rec	CCV4-TV	CCV4-Obs	CCV4-Rec	CCV5-TV	CCV5-Obs	CCV5-Rec
V (µ/L)	A	10	9.991375273	99.91375273	10	10.17824322	101.7824322	10	9.986948267	99.86948267
Cr	A	10	10.23747284	102.3747284	10	10.43125707	104.3125707	10	10.25176255	102.5176255
Mn	A	10	10.15512333	101.5512333	10	10.37120146	103.7120146	10	10.31078947	103.1078947
Fe	A	50.00000381	36.14374571	72.28748591	50.00000381	38.91393305	77.82786016	50.00000381	37.1038113	74.20761693
Ni	A	10	10.50028633	105.0028633	10	10.74240442	107.4240442	10	10.50248384	105.0248384
Cu	A	10	10.44103275	104.4103275	10	10.48291771	104.8291771	10	10.47122489	104.7122489
Zn	A	20	20.84492497	104.2246249	20	20.58320021	102.916011	20	20.72900602	103.6450301
As	A	10	10.07112922	100.7112922	10	10.2480377	102.480377	10	9.968211442	99.6821142
Cd	A	1	1.025773372	102.5773372	1	1.021258889	102.1258889	10	1.018553729	101.8553729
Sn	A		1.928422781			1.926497615			1.897775196	
Ba	A	10	9.859105991	98.59105991	10	9.892031641	98.92031641	10	9.646629084	96.48629084
Pb (µg/L)	A	2	2.169817453	108.4908727	2	2.173315751	108.6657876	2	2.166242576	108.3121288
THg (ng/L)	B	20	20.16609426	100.8304713	20	20.2686372	101.343186			

Analyte (unit)	Batch ID	CCV6-TV	CCV6-Obs	CCV6-Rec	CCV7-TV	CCV7-Obs	CCV7-Rec	CCV8-TV	CCV8-Obs	CCV8-Rec
V (µg/L)	A	10	9.849617357	98.49617357	10	9.783745819	97.83745819	10	9.586111375	95.86111375
Cr	A	10	10.1783771	101.783771	10	10.02781438	100.2781438	10	9.836530337	98.36530337
Mn	A	10	10.09998875	100.9998875	10	10.10092558	101.0092558	10	9.867526868	98.67526868
Fe	A	50.00000381	38.19419485	76.38838388	50.00000381	36.77596348	73.55192136	50.00000381	37.05366884	74.10733202
Ni	A	10	10.36700825	103.6700825	10	10.13588373	101.3588373	10	9.880873234	98.80873234
Cu	A	10	10.31545979	103.1545979	10	10.4797927	104.797927	10	10.41173962	104.1173962
Zn	A	20	20.23273385	101.1636692	20	21.04050314	105.2025157	20	20.66332202	103.3166101
As	A	10	9.847302208	98.47302208	10	9.983570755	99.83570755	10	9.73225454	97.3225454
Cd	A	1	1.002141532	100.2141532	1	1.031852437	103.1852437	1	0.985930772	98.59307716
Sn	A		1.887518769			1.858317909			1.881666636	
Ba	A	10	9.763108636	97.63108636	10	9.730458986	97.30458986	10	9.69027078	96.9027078
Pb (µg/L)	A	2	2.09613605	104.8068025	2	2.12493247	106.2466235	2	2.112768494	105.6384247
THg (ng/L)	B									

Table 3. (cont.)

Analyte (unit)	Batch ID	CCV9-TV	CCV9-Obs	CCV9-Rec	CCV10-TV	CCV10-Obs	CCV10-Rec	CCV11-TV	CCV11-Obs	CCV11-Rec
V (µg/L)	A	10	9.650594968	96.50594968	10	9.30736503	93.0736503	10	9.423536979	94.23536979
Cr	A	10	9.76573373	97.6573373	10	9.544484373	95.44484373	10	9.628965848	95.28965848
Mn	A	10	9.827188222	98.27188222	10	9.458645312	94.58645312	10	9.694133285	95.94133285
Fe	A	50.00000381	39.53449401	79.06898199	50.00000381	42.37362985	84.74725323	50.00000381	47.00665316	94.01329915
Ni	A	10	9.932683621	99.32683621	10	9.576026001	95.76026001	10	9.668495115	95.68495115
Cu	A	10	10.2025627	102.025627	10	9.890386321	98.90386321	10	10.0324925	100.324925
Zn	A	20	20.3137235	101.5686175	20	19.52618759	97.63093797	20	19.51674111	97.58370555
As	A	10	9.585721832	95.85721832	10	9.299644052	92.99644052	10	9.489074512	94.89074512
Cd	A	1	0.989542451	98.9542451	1	0.947602132	94.76021317	1	0.971535371	97.15353708
Sn	A		1.918633807			1.824633062			1.902547083	
Ba (µg/L)	A	10	9.838818362	98.38818362	10	9.148799712	91.48799712	10	9.62317503	96.2317503
Pb (µg/L)	A	2	2.12562117	106.2810585	2	2.025839268	101.2919634	2	2.117560977	105.8780489
THg (ng/L)	B									

Analyte (unit)	Batch ID	CCV12-TV	CCV12-Obs	CCV12-Rec	CCV13-TV	CCV13-Obs	CCV13-Rec	CCV14-TV	CCV14-Obs	CCV14-Rec
V (µg/L)	A	10	9.438779146	94.38779146	10	10.11357487	101.1357487	10	10.02901924	100.2901924
Cr	A	10	9.5126383	95.126383	10	10.31263132	103.1263132	10	10.23583896	102.3583896
Mn	A	10	9.651176105	96.51176105	10	10.29423463	102.9423463	10	10.19991661	101.9991661
Fe	A	50.00000381	53.94851826	107.8970283	50.00000381	43.16024445	86.32048232	50.00000381	38.81284795	77.62568998
Ni	A	10	9.577118118	95.77118118	10	10.4172239	104.172239	10	10.22561713	102.2561713
Cu	A	10	9.803673602	98.03673602	10	10.22385582	102.2385582	10	10.20193347	102.0193347
Zn	A	20	19.1865418	95.93270898	20	20.44292065	102.2146032	20	20.36064296	101.8032148
As	A	10	9.149850875	91.49850875	10	9.69797573	96.9797573	10	9.683501646	96.83501646
Cd	A	1	0.947509367	94.75093668	1	1.017795471	101.7795471	1	0.993801395	99.38013952
Sn	A		1.87476249			1.934516221			1.935159194	
Ba (µg/L)	A	10	9.423369849	94.23369849	10	9.725311342	97.25311342	10	9.599800774	95.99800774
Pb (µg/L)	A	2	2.101084924	105.0542462	2	2.142351295	107.1175648	2	2.113897098	105.6948549
THg (ng/L)	B									

Table 4: Results of the QA/QC analysis concerning calibration blanks.

Analyte (unit)	Batch ID	ICB	CCB1	CCB2	CCB3	CCB4	CCB5	CCB6	CCB7
V (µg/L)	A	-0.019412662	-0.022915678	0.003640651	0.017759003	0.048708424	0.023439894	0.02438426	0.002141815
Cr	A	-0.002122966	0.003766614	0.010165725	-0.002818597	-0.009003925	-0.023367497	-0.030559529	-0.051678352
Mn	A	0.001514224	-0.000366763	0.001696906	0.000215278	0.001268211	-0.000454617	0.00102575	0.000273924
Fe	A	-1.281956901	2.199543674	2.977579904	2.51391155	1.110781557	0.8398272	0.879905186	-1.557955314
Ni	A	0.006692471	0.001049361	0.003343839	0.001642198	0.001944399	0.002645204	0.001884406	0.003968292
Cu	A	-0.002534501	-0.01197791	-0.016823747	-0.010802005	-0.007336244	-0.00454008	-0.005354424	-0.010948432
Zn	A	0.009717066	-0.00744 2436	0.000322795	0.006762036	-0.006444729	0.008655965	0.006723209	-0.002946931
As	A	0.03487219	0.023736137	0.056976428	0.045339725	0.040974748	0.038955845	0.078805291	0.045033425
Cd	A	0.001390389	0.00066378	8.54564E-05	0.000269234	-0.000194387	0.000389272	-0.000239253	-9.69004E-05
Sn	A	0.247473511	0.019964263	0.023887361	0.026699068	0.02564591	0.020272009	0.02815594	0.027853262
Ba	A	0.010189992	0.001502795	0.000655891	0.000560007	0.001351205	0.001324258	0.002003348	0.00180285
Pb (µg/L)	A	0.000486244	0.000574009	0.000689952	0.000983047	0.000643604	0.00057415	0.000284386	-9.19744E-05
THg (ng/L)	B	0.005127147	0.010254294	0.020508588	0.076907204	0.061525765			

Analyte (unit)	Batch ID	CCB8	CCB9	CCB10	CCB11	CCB12	CCB13	CCB14
V (µg/L)	A	-0.010947072	-0.016725359	0.011709312	0.027295459	0.010289739	-0.013957262	-0.006775751
Cr	A	-0.056714697	-0.075768997	-0.066915037	-0.094584515	-0.116960163	-0.131259752	-0.112840693
Mn	A	-0.001074566	0.002161963	0.03136897	0.054314014	0.051490255	0.01542742	0.016643044
Fe	A	2.653762053	2.800329156	9.014763907	14.93157478	8.144938152	1.341967988	1.754123921
Ni	A	0.012223274	0.01125807	0.033918849	0.047015877	0.046362983	0.063122249	0.068449487
Cu	A	-0.008492945	-0.000696379	0.013466952	0.027762757	0.027535099	0.006185382	0.006529685
Zn	A	0.033953836	0.038064624	0.099442749	0.102272735	0.1616685	1.112588417	1.239113157
As	A	0.061924645	0.084226575	0.115874334	0.115621475	0.148838907	0.073167584	0.093352707
Cd	A	-1.18679E-05	0.000420587	0.002093238	0.003724701	0.004472952	0.000266891	0.001259444
Sn	A	0.020168967	0.01414789	0.033233545	0.026029557	0.025150975	0.013041776	0.013497487
Ba	A	0.000679496	0.001074303	0.025160283	0.044806803	0.045522298	0.011303463	0.011303808
Pb (µg/L)	A	-0.000259981	-0.000394815	0.004911209	0.009329379	0.009550545	0.005268769	0.005122446
THg (ng/L)	B							

Table 5: Results of the QA/QC analysis concerning spikes.

Analyte (unit)	Batch ID	Sample ID	Mean	Spike TV	Dup Spike TV	Obs Spike Value	Dup Obs Spike Value	Spike % Rec	Dup Spike % Rec	RPD
V (mg/kg)	A	BL03-4	87.22	98.81	98.81	190.0	190.8	104.0	104.8	0.7
V	A	BL03-3	126.6	79.37	79.68	205.3	207.9	99.1	102.0	2.9
Cr	A	BL03-4	55.07	98.81	98.81	157.7	158.3	103.8	104.4	0.6
Cr	A	BL03-3	72.52	79.37	79.68	145.8	142.0	92.3	87.2	5.7
Mn	A	BL03-4	1215	98.81	98.81	1324	1324	110.4	109.6	0.8
Mn	A	BL03-3	312.4	79.37	79.68	385.4	394.4	92.1	102.9	11.1
Fe	A	BL03-3	30902	79.37	79.68	32448	30620	1949	−353.9	288.8
Fe	A	BL03-4	21899	494.1	494.1	22701	22647	162.3	151.4	6.9
Ni	A	BL03-3	40.88	79.37	79.68	124.0	126.3	104.8	107.2	2.3
Ni	A	BL03-4	27.48	123.5	123.5	154.7	156.6	103.0	104.5	1.4
Cu	A	BL03-4	20.40	123.5	123.5	148.1	146.4	103.4	102.0	1.4
Cu	A	BL03-3	42.67	79.37	79.68	127.3	128.1	106.7	107.2	0.5
Zn	A	BL03-3	111.6	79.37	79.68	187.8	188.3	96.1	96.3	0.2
Zn	A	BL03-4	60.59	247.0	247.0	311.7	313.3	101.6	102.3	0.6
As	A	BL03-3	18.48	79.37	79.68	91.56	92.81	92.1	93.3	1.3
As	A	BL03-4	9.84	98.81	98.81	113.1	111.9	104.5	103.3	1.1
Cd	A	BL03-3	0.229	79.37	79.68	76.35	76.99	95.9	96.3	0.4
Cd	A	BL03-4	0.196	9.881	9.881	10.47	10.27	103.9	101.9	2.0
Sn	A	BL03-3	1.774	79.37	79.68	80.55	79.81	99.3	97.9	1.3
Sn	A	BL03-4	1.523	24.70	24.70	27.54	26.69	105.3	101.9	3.3
Ba	A	BL03-3	497.2	79.37	79.68	596.7	521.8	125.4	30.9	120.9
Ba	A	BL03-4	357.1	197.6	197.6	578.6	576.8	112.1	111.2	0.8
Pb	A	BL03-3	19.08	79.37	79.68	98.77	98.35	100.4	99.5	0.9
Pb (mg/kg)	A	BL03-4	11.04	24.70	24.70	35.68	35.48	99.7	99.0	0.8
THg (ng/g)	B	BL03-4	12.62	48.75	50.20	59.84	61.63	96.9	97.6	0.8

Table 6: Results of the QA/QC analysis concerning replicates (precision determination).

Analyte (unit)	Batch ID	Sample ID	Sample	Duplicate	Mean	RPD
V (mg/kg)	A	BL03-4	87.28	87.17	87.22	0.1
V	A	BL03-3	127.0	126.2	126.6	0.6
Cr	A	BL03-4	55.46	54.68	55.07	1.4
Cr	A	BL03-3	72.70	72.35	72.52	0.5
Mn	A	BL03-4	1222	1209	1215	1.1
Mn	A	BL03-3	310.5	314.3	312.4	1.2
Fe	A	BL03-3	30998	30805	30902	0.6
Fe	A	BL03-4	22087	21711	21899	1.7
Ni	A	BL03-3	40.63	41.13	40.88	1.2
Ni	A	BL03-4	27.23	27.74	27.48	1.8
Cu	A	BL03-4	19.87	20.94	20.40	5.3
Cu	A	BL03-3	42.27	43.07	42.67	1.9
Zn	A	BL03-3	110.4	112.8	111.6	2.1
Zn	A	BL03-4	60.21	60.96	60.59	1.2
As	A	BL03-3	18.36	18.60	18.48	1.3
As	A	BL03-4	9.97	9.71	9.84	2.6
Cd	A	BL03-3	0.233	0.225	0.229	3.4
Cd	A	BL03-4	0.196	0.196	0.196	0.2
Sn	A	BL03-3	1.76	1.79	1.77	1.6
Sn	A	BL03-4	1.53	1.51	1.52	1.1
Ba	A	BL03-3	511.6	482.8	497.2	5.8
Ba	A	BL03-4	355.0	359.2	357.1	1.2
Pb	A	BL03-3	19.10	19.05	19.08	0.2
Pb (mg/kg)	A	BL03-4	11.03	11.05	11.04	0.2
THg (ng/g)	B	BL03-4	11.68	13.56	12.62	14.9
% Total Solids	C	BL03-4	79.5	78.9	79.2	0.8
% Total Solids	C	BL03-17	79.6	79.5	79.6	0.1

Table 7: Results of the QA/QC analysis concerning analytical accuracy using certified reference materials, NIST 2709 and IAEA 405.

Analyte (unit)	Batch ID	CRM Identity	Cert Value	Obs Value	% Rec
V (mg/kg)	A	NIST 2709	112.00	97.12	86.7
V	A	BlankSpike	80.00	85.78	107.2
V	A	IAEA 405	95.00	90.21	95.0
Cr	A	IAEA 405	84.00	67.42	80.3
Cr	A	BlankSpike	80.00	86.14	107.7
Cr	A	NIST 2709	130.00	93.28	71.8
Mn	A	NIST 2709	538.00	420.18	78.1
Mn	A	IAEA 405	495.00	384.99	77.8
Mn	A	BlankSpike	80.00	87.95	109.9
Fe	A	BlankSpike	80.00	58.29	72.9
Fe	A	NIST 2709	35000.00	28463.83	81.3
Fe	A	IAEA 405	37400.00	29885.25	79.9
Ni	A	IAEA 405	32.50	32.42	99.8
Ni	A	BlankSpike	80.00	93.66	117.1
Ni	A	NIST 2709	88.00	76.19	86.6
Cu	A	BlankSpike	80.00	89.09	111.4
Cu	A	NIST 2709	34.60	37.34	107.9
Cu	A	IAEA 405	47.70	54.28	113.8
Zn	A	IAEA 405	279.00	281.40	100.9
Zn	A	NIST 2709	106.00	106.90	100.8
Zn	A	BlankSpike	80.00	83.51	104.4
As	A	NIST 2709	17.70	16.84	95.1
As	A	IAEA 405	23.60	23.47	99.5
As	A	BlankSpike	80.00	75.32	94.2
Cd	A	BlankSpike	80.00	78.38	98.0
Cd	A	NIST 2709	0.38	0.65	172.1
Cd	A	IAEA 405	0.73	0.74	101.8
Sn	A	IAEA 405	7.60	9.54	125.5
Sn	A	BlankSpike	80.00	79.93	99.9
Ba	A	NIST 2709	968.00	845.36	87.3
Ba	A	BlankSpike	80.00	97.11	121.4
Pb	A	NIST 2709	18.90	19.29	102.1
Pb	A	IAEA 405	74.80	77.83	104.0
Pb (mg/kg)	A	BlankSpike	80.00	78.63	98.3
THg (ng/g)	B	IAEA 405	810.00	765.78	94.5

Table 8: Correlation coefficients for chemical and physical parameters of muds from Beaufort Lagoon (N = 19; significant correlations [p <0.05] are shown in bold and insignificant correlations are in gray).

	V	Cr	Mn	Ni	Cu	Zn	As	Cd	Sn	Ba	Pb	Fe	OC %	Silt %	Clay %
V	1.00														
Cr	0.89	1.00													
Mn	0.07	-0.07	1.00												
Ni	0.85	0.71	0.48	1.00											
Cu	0.80	0.64	0.39	0.91	1.00										
Zn	0.84	0.78	-0.16	0.69	0.76	1.00									
As	0.72	0.52	0.12	0.55	0.58	0.68	1.00								
Cd	0.41	0.54	0.30	0.57	0.45	0.45	0.31	1.00							
Sn	0.48	0.43	0.74	0.78	0.61	0.35	0.40	0.78	1.00						
Ba	0.53	0.57	-0.38	0.31	0.47	0.70	0.26	0.08	-0.12	1.00					
Pb	0.70	0.50	0.80	0.89	0.92	0.58	0.68	0.63	0.86	0.10	1.00				
Fe	0.73	0.85	0.28	0.58	0.62	0.77	0.71	0.59	0.50	0.48	0.70	1.00			
OC %	0.37	0.40	0.12	0.42	0.31	0.62	0.44	0.66	0.46	0.07	0.38	0.44	1.00		
Silt %	-0.63	-0.40	-0.75	-0.81	-0.73	-0.51	-0.72	-0.73	-0.93	0.19	-0.88	-0.52	-0.44	1.00	
Clay %	0.64	0.40	0.74	0.82	0.75	0.55	0.72	0.72	0.93	-0.17	0.88	0.52	0.58	-1.00	1.00

Table 9: Time-interval changes in the mean concentrations (µg/g dry wt) of trace metals in sediments of Beaufort Lagoon.[a]

Year	V	Cr	Mn	Ni	Cu	Zi
1977[b]						
N=5						
$\overline{X}$	**139**	69	**359**	48	**22**	81
SD	17	12	69	6	4	11
CV%	12	17	19	13	18	14
2003[c]						
N=21						
$\overline{X}$	**119**	73	**472**	39	**36**	92
SD	13	7	659	7	9	17
CV%	11	10	139	18	25	19

[a]Significant differences (p<0.05) in bold
[b]Naidu [1981]
[c]This study (Table 2)

46

Table 10: Distribution (ng/g dry wt) of *n*-alkanes in gross sediments of Beaufort Lagoon. All sample numbers have the prefix BL03.

Sample ID – UCLA No.	1	2	3	3D*	4	4R*	5B	6B	9	9B	9BD*	10	11A	12
Surrogate Recovery (%)														
Deu C14	nd$	52	52	53	56	57	53	55	52	62	62	52	55	53
Deu C24	nd$	66	67	69	69	64	70	63	65	76	76	76	66	67
Deu C36	nd$	67	78	75	61	66	72	65	66	66	79	66	65	67
n-alkane (ng/g dry wt)														
n-C10	nd	nd	nd	nd	nd	nd	nd	nd	nd	nd	nd	nd	nd	nd
n-C11	nd	nd	nd	nd	nd	nd	62.9	217.6	nd	nd	nd	nd	nd	nd
n-C12	nd	nd	nd	nd	nd	nd	nd	nd	nd	nd	nd	nd	nd	nd
n-C13	nd	nd	nd	nd	nd	nd	nd	nd	nd	nd	nd	nd	nd	38.9
n-C14	nd	nd	nd	nd	nd	nd	nd	nd	nd	nd	nd	nd	nd	46.9
n-C15	67.1	34.4	60.7	52.6	nd	nd	38.7	72.3	45.5	41.1	30.7	0.0	55.1	70.9
n-C16	96.2	26.0	56.6	41.9	nd	nd	32.8	62.5	56.9	50.9	40.5	0.0	58.9	77.4
n-C17	184.3	70.9	192.5	172.5	3.2	3.8	117.0	198.8	192.8	98.5	76.0	51.6	137.6	163.6
pr	nd	nd	nd	nd	nd	nd	nd	nd	nd	nd	nd	nd	nd	51.6
n-C18	89.6	38.2	108.7	98.0	1.8	2.2	63.5	110.4	102.0	54.3	46.2	29.4	76.8	95.0
ph	nd	nd	nd	nd	nd	nd	nd	nd	nd	nd	nd	nd	nd	nd
n-C19	280.1	99.8	317.3	287.4	3.8	4.6	181.5	307.2	321.8	162.1	140.2	73.9	215.4	231.6
n-C20	166.5	65.2	198.8	180.4	2.8	3.4	116.9	202.4	191.1	110.5	96.5	52.3	148.5	167.6
n-C21	579.0	204.2	630.6	584.7	7.3	7.5	382.1	627.9	623.2	360.7	316.3	162.5	496.3	501.2
n-C22	312.8	116.1	323.6	311.7	5.1	5.7	196.5	332.7	330.7	196.8	180.1	91.0	285.4	292.6
n-C23	990.9	354.0	1056.6	974.1	13.2	14.9	672.8	1068.7	995.0	676.7	605.0	302.1	943.3	948.8
n-C24	268.7	105.7	287.0	294.6	5.6	6.0	186.8	318.7	305.5	188.1	184.1	86.3	277.8	279.1
n-C25	826.3	341.2	839.9	814.5	14.9	14.6	573.5	951.2	819.1	735.8	661.7	318.9	1403.9	1126.0
n-C26	126.6	58.2	153.8	146.9	3.9	3.6	103.0	178.8	146.2	112.4	109.5	48.8	155.5	162.3
n-C27	1015.9	472.0	1483.4	1450.0	18.1	18.5	867.3	1239.8	1738.7	1496.4	1370.4	460.7	1817.5	1985.2
n-C28	73.3	34.5	94.5	176.6	3.5	3.4	70.0	120.0	80.1	81.0	144.5	33.3	110.7	108.0
n-C29	886.5	376.5	1217.9	1346.5	17.9	18.6	933.4	1323.9	1054.3	1160.3	1450.2	414.2	1342.7	1413.3
n-C30	83.2	29.9	128.9	141.1	3.6	2.8	79.0	129.8	35.0	100.8	116.7	38.8	126.0	128.2
n-C31	749.0	308.8	1190.4	1330.8	18.4	18.4	889.2	1312.5	938.5	988.7	1152.2	378.4	1201.3	1269.8
n-C32	146.2	46.7	82.0	39.4	1.8	2.0	49.0	86.0	41.5	68.5	39.2	39.9	85.4	41.5
n-C33	210.3	90.1	378.7	444.7	7.1	7.1	274.4	424.7	264.6	300.5	375.4	119.7	377.4	407.1
n-C34	nd	26.7	58.2	63.3	2.4	2.0	nd	67.6	80.1	nd	47.9	nd	nd	71.0
n-C35	nd	nd	nd	44.7	2.0	2.6	nd	nd	nd	nd	nd	nd	nd	nd
n-C36	nd	nd	nd	nd	nd	nd	nd	nd	nd	nd	nd	nd	nd	nd
Total n-alkanes (ng/g dry wt)	7152.4	2899.1	8860.1	8996.4	136.5	142.0	5890.2	9353.3	8362.6	6984.2	7183.3	2701.9	9315.4	9625.9
Σ C12–C19 (ng/g dry wt)	717.3	269.4	735.9	652.3	8.8	10.7	433.5	751.2	719.0	407.0	333.5	155.0	543.7	724.4
Σ C20–C33 (ng/dry wt)	6435.1	2603.0	8066.0	8236.0	123.2	126.7	5393.8	8316.9	7563.5	6577.3	6801.8	2546.9	8771.7	8830.5
Pr/Ph	nd	nd	nd	nd	nd	nd	nd	nd	nd	nd	nd	nd	nd	nd
Odd/Even**	4.2	4.3	4.9	5.0	3.5	3.5	5.5	4.7	5.1	6.3	6.1	5.4	6.0	5.7

Table 10. (cont.)

Sample ID – UCLA No.	13	14	15	16	17	18	19	20	OS#	Pr. Blk	XSPIKE 1 % Recovery	XSPIKE 2 % Recovery	XSPIKE % Rec Avg
Surrogate Recovery (%)													
Deu C14	57	55	58	nd$	53	58	60	54	nd$	51	52	52	52
Deu C24	76	64	61	nd$	65	68	61	66	nd$	57	64	66	65
Deu C36	80	65	58	nd$	92	70	65	68	nd$	66	74	72	73
n-alkane (ng/g dry wt)									µg/g dry wt				
n-C10	nd	nd	nd	nd	nd	nd	25.4	nd	499.6	nd	18	19	19
n-C11	nd	nd	nd	nd	nd	nd	34.2	nd	3761.2	nd	28	22	25
n-C12	nd	nd	nd	nd	nd	nd	17.3	nd	489.6	nd	33	35	34
n-C13	nd	32.2	nd	nd	nd	nd	nd	nd	253.8	nd	40	41	41
n-C14	nd	27.2	nd	nd	nd	nd	nd	nd	148.3	nd	50	50	50
n-C15	74.2	66.1	nd	nd	2.7	31.7	14.9	17.0	65.0	nd	57	58	57
n-C16	55.7	53.9	nd	223.8	2.0	31.4	15.2	9.6	nd	nd	66	64	65
n-C17	170.8	144.6	75.4	754.9	5.7	103.6	66.4	37.1	nd	nd	65	68	67
pr	nd	38.7	nd	nd	nd	13.1	7.7	nd	nd	nd	67	68	67
n-C18	94.4	80.1	41.0	339.8	3.9	58.9	37.5	19.1	nd	nd	69	69	69
ph	nd	18.4	nd	nd	nd	nd	nd	nd	nd	nd	69	69	69
n-C19	36.0	208.0	103.7	1141.0	1.9	174.1	122.4	62.6	nd	nd	70	70	70
n-C20	146.1	147.8	73.7	680.8	5.3	112.2	76.4	36.1	58.1	nd	72	72	72
n-C21	421.2	464.0	227.0	2275.8	13.9	364.2	246.9	109.3	86.9	nd	72	72	72
n-C22	36.9	260.3	138.3	1238.2	7.5	199.6	127.8	61.3	53.2	nd	76	72	74
n-C23	831.6	834.4	444.2	4079.3	20.6	630.8	400.8	167.0	67.6	nd	69	66	68
n-C24	35.0	250.1	142.8	1116.4	6.9	186.7	112.7	51.3	71.8	nd	60	63	62
n-C25	911.3	888.6	491.9	3918.1	19.4	556.5	349.5	136.0	218.4	nd	65	69	67
n-C26	191.3	124.6	86.3	574.5	4.2	100.5	52.0	27.0	87.9	nd	70	69	70
n-C27	1608.1	1718.1	863.0	5131.4	20.6	1085.1	369.4	146.4	179.1	nd	69	70	69
n-C28	159.2	97.3	65.5	328.6	3.1	64.3	26.1	15.5	60.2	nd	66	70	68
n-C29	1628.0	1538.0	682.9	4763.2	25.7	855.6	325.2	143.7	138.0	nd	66	67	67
n-C30	149.4	98.4	60.2	334.1	2.2	93.1	41.0	20.4	230.1	nd	66	65	66
n-C31	1621.1	1150.4	600.7	4488.1	25.2	861.2	339.9	156.5	171.2	nd	67	64	66
n-C32	68.6	32.3	0.0	784.7	0.0	26.2	15.1	11.8	169.6	nd	64	69	66
n-C33	564.4	354.9	195.2	1339.2	8.3	271.3	110.5	51.0	nd	nd	66	63	64
n-C34	49.4	52.6	nd	330.4	nd	45.8	29.9	13.5	nd	nd	64	62	63
n-C35	75.2	30.2	nd	nd	nd	24.4	10.9	nd	nd	nd	60	63	62
n-C36	nd	nd	nd	nd	nd	nd	nd	nd	nd	nd	69	69	69
Total n-alkanes (ng/g dry wt)	8927.9	8654.2	4291.7	33842.3	179.2	5877.3	2967.7	1292.1	6819.4				
Σ C12–C19 (ng/g dry wt)	431.1	612.2	220.1	2459.5	16.1	399.7	273.8	145.3	956.6				
Σ C20–C33 (ng/g dry wt)	8372.3	7959.2	4071.7	31052.4	163.1	5407.4	2593.5	1133.3	1602.1				
Pr/Ph	nd	2.1	nd	nd	nd	na†	na†	nd	nd				
Odd/Even**	8.1	6.2	6.1	4.7	4.1	5.4	4.4	3.9	1.3				

* Duplicate (D) or replicate (R) analysis
** Summed n-C15–n-C36
# OS=oil spill sample; note change in units of concentration
nd$=dilution too great to measure surrogates
nd=not detected
na†=not applicable, phytane not detected

48

Table 11: Distribution (ng/g dry wt) of PAHs in gross sediments of Beaufort Lagoon. All lagoon sample numbers have the prefix BL03.

Sample ID – UCLA No.	1	2	3	3D*	4	5B	6B
Surrogate Recovery (%)							
hexamethylbenzene	62	53	50	50	38	41	44
n-dodecylbenzene	57	58	62	64	59	59	60
4-terphenyl-D14	64	60	75	68	68	65	57
PAH (ng g⁻¹ dry wt)							
naphthalene	7.7	7.4	13.0	16.7	nd	7.3	6.7
C1-naphthalenes	18.9	21.3	26.3	27.2	nd	15.4	21.4
2-methylnaphthalene	10.0	10.7	14.8	14.9	nd	6.4	12.1
1-methylnaphthalene	8.9	10.6	11.6	12.4	nd	9.0	9.4
C2-naphthalenes	27.1	33.3	41.6	48.2	0.4	28.9	50.0
2,6-dimethylnaphthalene	8.0	8.5	6.9	7.5	nd	5.6	16.0
C3-naphthalenes	14.7	26.8	34.1	37.8	0.5	13.8	39.6
2,3,5-trimethylnaphthalene	nd	4.4	6.1	7.0	nd	2.4	3.8
C4-naphthalenes	1.7	12.0	17.9	19.8	nd	7.0	18.9
biphenyl	5.6	4.3	9.2	9.9	nd	4.9	7.1
acenaphthylene	nd	nd	nd	nd	nd	nd	nd
acenaphthene	nd	0.6	0.9	1.1	nd	nd	nd
fluorene	nd	2.9	4.9	5.1	nd	2.7	5.4
2-methylfluorene	nd	2.7	4.3	5.1	nd	nd	nd
C1-fluorenes	3.2	3.8	6.4	nd	tr	2.8	5.8
C2-fluorenes	4.9	6.7	13.3	nd	tr	6.4	18.6
C3-fluorenes	tr	tr	nd	nd	nd	tr	tr
phenanthrene	19.5	15.2	27.8	32.0	1.1	17.9	33.4
1-methylphenanthrene	4.4	4.9	6.7	7.5	nd	3.4	8.8
anthracene	1.6	nd	1.3	1.3	nd	nd	nd
C1-phenanthrenes/anthracenes	47.9	51.3	72.5	77.1	20.8	34.6	123.2
C2-phenanthrenes/anthracenes	12.8	26.7	32.6	35.7	1.8	19.4	57.5
3,6-dimethylphenanthrene	nd	1.2	3.7	4.2	nd	nd	1.8
C3-phenanthrenes/anthracenes	18.0	23.7	43.7	46.6	4.7	22.2	58.3
C4-phenanthrenes/anthracenes	5.2	10.9	17.0	17.5	1.0	9.5	28.0
2,3-benzofluorene	nd	1.6	2.5	3.2	nd	1.3	2.9
1,1'-binaphthalene	nd	nd	nd	nd	nd	nd	nd
d benzothiophene**	nd	3.4	5.4	7.6	0.2	3.4	6.7
C1-dibenzothiophenes**	2.5	3.5	3.5	3.8	0.3	2.1	6.3
C2-dibenzothiophenes**	2.6	4.6	6.1	6.6	nd	2.9	12.0
C3-dibenzothiophenes**	5.9	23.7	6.5	6.8	nd	1.8	6.8
C4-dibenzothiophenes**	nd	tr	1.8	1.9	nd	nd	nd
fluoranthene	3.8	2.7	4.1	4.3	nd	2.5	5.6
pyrene	5.7	4.9	7.6	8.6	0.6	4.4	9.6
C1-fluoranthenes/pyrenes	3.8	4.2	6.8	7.1	tr	4.3	10.8
C2-fluoranthenes/pyrenes	7.5	7.2	7.9	8.1	tr	7.2	12.8

PAH (ng g⁻¹ dry wt) (cont.)	1	2	3	3D*	4	5B	6B
C3-fluoranthenes/pyrenes	4.9	2.6	2.2	2.3	nd	1.3	5.2
C4-fluoranthenes/pyrenes	nd	1.7	3.3	3.6	nd	tr	6.3
benz(a)anthracene	4.0	1.4	2.7	3.7	0.5	1.3	3.9
chrysene/triphenylene	12.0	8.0	14.8	15.3	0.8	9.5	19.4
C1-chrysenes/triphenylenes	7.9	9.2	12.5	13.0	tr	7.6	18.9
C2-chrysenes/triphenylenes	2.6	4.3	6.0	6.4	nd	1.0	8.1
C3-chrysenes/triphenylenes	tr	tr	nd	nd	nd	nd	nd
C4-chrysenes/triphenylenes	nd	nd	nd	nd	nd	nd	nd
benzo(k)fluoranthene	3.8	1.0	1.0	1.1	0.3	0.5	1.8
benzo(b)fluoranthene	7.6	4.5	8.0	8.5	0.5	6.8	13.3
benzo(e)pyrene	9.2	5.6	8.1	8.8	0.5	5.4	12.0
benzo(a)pyrene	3.8	1.6	1.6	1.9	0.2	1.5	1.7
9,10-diphenylanthracene	nd	nd	nd	nd	nd	nd	nd
perylene	30.3	35.9	42.5	43.1	2.6	22.1	53.4
indeno(1,2,3-cd)pyrene	nd	nd	nd	nd	nd	nd	nd
d benz(a,h)anthracene	nd	nd	nd	nd	nd	nd	nd
picene	nd	nd	nd	nd	nd	nd	nd
benzo(ghi)perylene	nd	3.6	4.6	5.0	nd	nd	nd
anthanthrene	nd	nd	nd	nd	nd	nd	nd
coronene	nd	nd	nd	nd	nd	nd	nd
1,2,4,5-d benzopyrene	nd	nd	nd	nd	nd	nd	nd
C1-C20H12 aromatics	9.5	5.1	6.9	7.2	nd	5.5	15.3
C2-C20H12 aromatics	tr	1.7	2.6	2.7	nd	1.0	2.9
C3-C20H12 aromatics	nd	tr	nd	nd	nd	nd	nd
C4-C20H12 aromatics	nd	tr	nd	nd	nd	nd	nd
sum-naphthalenes(N)	70.1	100.9	132.9	149.6	0.9	72.3	136.7
sum-fluorenes(F)	8.1	13.4	24.6	5.1	nd	11.9	29.8
sum-phenanthrenes/anthracenes(PA)	105.1	127.9	194.8	210.2	29.3	103.6	300.5
sum-dibenzothiophenes(D)	11.0	35.2	23.3	26.7	0.6	10.2	31.8
sum-fluoranthenes/pyrenes(FP)	25.8	23.2	31.8	33.9	0.6	19.7	50.3
sum-chrysenes(C)	22.5	21.5	33.3	34.7	0.8	18.2	46.4
sum-C20H12 aromatics(C20)	64.2	55.2	70.6	73.4	4.1	42.9	100.3
sum-4,5 PAH (4,5 PAH)	107.0	94.6	128.9	135.8	6.0	75.4	182.7
sum-PAH(t-PAH)	316.4	388.8	531.3	556.7	36.7	286.3	709.7
N/PA	0.67	0.79	0.68	0.71	0.03	0.70	0.46
N/perylene	2.31	2.81	3.13	3.47	0.34	3.26	2.56
F/perylene	0.27	0.37	0.58	0.12	nd	0.54	0.56
PA/perylene	3.47	3.56	4.59	4.88	11.16	4.68	5.62
FP/perylene	0.85	0.65	0.75	0.79	0.22	0.89	0.94
t-PAH/perylene	10.45	10.83	12.51	12.92	13.99	12.93	13.29

49

Table 11. (cont.)

Sample ID – UCLA No.	9	9B	10	11A	12	13	14
Surrogate Recovery (%)							
hexamethylbenzene	46	43	39	44	40	40	45
n-dodecylbenzene	66	50	59	62	56	56	59
4-terphenyl-D14	72	63	72	63	69	69	71
PAH (ng/g dry wt)							
naphthalene	8.3	7.6	1.7	8.9	3.3	1.0	9.7
C1-naphthalenes	19.2	12.4	4.4	26.4	18.2	4.6	25.9
2-methylnaphthalene	9.7	7.0	2.5	13.8	9.3	2.7	14.8
1-methylnaphthalene	9.5	5.5	2.0	12.7	8.9	1.9	11.2
C2-naphthalenes	23.3	19.5	7.8	42.7	46.9	9.4	46.7
2,6-dimethylnaphthalene	7.3	6.2	2.0	14.4	12.9	2.5	12.1
C3-naphthalenes	16.5	13.6	7.7	33.0	40.1	7.4	34.0
2,3,5-trimethylnaphthalene	3.0	nd	nd	3.1	4.2	0.9	4.1
C4-naphthalenes	7.0	6.5	2.6	13.1	16.1	4.6	18.4
biphenyl	4.5	4.8	1.3	7.2	4.7	1.5	5.9
acenaphthylene	nd	nd	nd	nd	nd	nd	nd
acenaphthene	nd	nd	nd	nd	nd	nd	nd
fluorene	2.5	2.6	nd	4.3	4.0	1.1	4.0
2-methylfluorene	nd	nd	nd	nd	3.1	0.8	3.0
C1-fluorenes	3.5	3.1	1.2	5.3	5.5	1.2	6.3
C2-fluorenes	6.0	5.6	2.6	15.0	13.1	1.9	13.1
C3-fluorenes	tr	tr	tr	tr	tr	tr	tr
phenanthrene	14.9	17.3	5.3	24.0	25.1	6.4	21.3
1-methylphenanthrene	3.1	5.1	1.6	6.7	8.0	1.9	6.5
anthracene	nd	nd	nd	nd	nd	nd	nd
C1-phenanthrenes/anthracenes	25.9	37.2	41.5	112.8	138.0	56.6	193.7
C2-phenanthrenes/anthracenes	15.9	18.1	10.0	36.0	52.7	11.9	47.3
3,6-dimethylphenanthrene	1.2	1.2	0.4	1.8	1.8	0.4	1.9
C3-phenanthrenes/anthracenes	15.0	14.1	17.2	63.7	82.7	21.4	100.4
C4-phenanthrenes/anthracenes	6.3	7.8	5.4	20.3	18.6	6.4	22.9
2,3-benzofluorene	1.1	nd	0.3	2.1	2.6	nd	2.1
1,1'-binaphthalene	nd	nd	nd	nd	nd	nd	nd
d benzothiophene	3.5	3.3	1.0	5.0	nd	1.4	3.7
C1-dibenzothiophenes**	2.1	1.8	1.5	4.4	6.5	1.5	6.0
C2-dibenzothiophenes**	3.1	1.2	1.2	6.3	8.5	nd	4.1
C3-dibenzothiophenes**	8.0	nd	0.7	4.2	8.4	nd	3.1
C4-dibenzothiophenes**	tr	nd	nd	nd	nd	nd	nd
fluoranthene	3.2	2.4	0.9	4.1	5.1	1.2	3.7
pyrene	4.6	4.8	1.5	6.5	8.5	2.1	7.6
C1-fluoranthenes/pyrenes	3.0	3.4	1.7	6.7	8.0	2.3	7.6
C2-fluoranthenes/pyrenes	3.1	7.8	2.6	7.7	11.4	2.5	8.8

PAH (ng/g dry wt) (cont.)	9	9B	10	11A	12	13	14
C3-fluoranthenes/pyrenes	1.6	2.9	1.3	2.0	3.7	1.0	3.6
C4-fluoranthenes/pyrenes	nd	3.2	1.1	nd	tr	nd	1.9
benz(a)anthracene	1.8	1.7	0.6	1.6	2.0	0.9	2.1
chrysene/triphenylene	9.3	8.9	3.3	12.3	15.6	3.9	12.8
C1-chrysenes/triphenylenes	6.7	6.8	2.4	12.4	18.5	3.2	14.6
C2-chrysenes/triphenylenes	1.9	2.4	0.9	4.8	12.4	tr	6.0
C3-chrysenes/triphenylenes	nd	nd	nd	3.8	tr	nd	nd
C4-chrysenes/triphenylenes	nd	nd	nd	nd	tr	nd	nd
benzo(k)fluoranthene	nd	0.6	0.3	1.1	1.3	0.4	1.2
benzo(b)fluoranthene	4.7	5.3	2.1	7.0	8.5	2.2	9.6
benzo(e)pyrene	4.1	4.8	2.0	5.9	9.6	2.5	7.5
benzo(a)pyrene	nd	nd	0.4	nd	nd	nd	nd
9,10-diphenylanthracene	nd	nd	nd	nd	nd	nd	nd
perylene	15.6	79.8	13.7	32.5	44.8	16.5	20.3
indeno(1,2,3-cd)pyrene	nd	nd	nd	nd	nd	nd	nd
d benz(a,h)anthracene	nd	nd	nd	nd	nd	nd	nd
picene	nd	nd	nd	nd	nd	nd	nd
benzo(ghi)perylene	nd	nd	nd	4.8	7.6	nd	nd
anthanthrene	nd	nd	nd	nd	nd	nd	nd
coronene	nd	nd	nd	nd	nd	nd	nd
1,2,4,5-d benzopyrene	nd	nd	nd	nd	nd	nd	nd
C1-C20H12 aromatics	2.7	4.4	3.1	4.6	2.2	3.1	4.3
C2-C20H12 aromatics	nd	3.7	0.7	tr	tr	nd	2.2
C3-C20H12 aromatics	nd	nd	nd	tr	nd	nd	nd
C4-C20H12 aromatics	nd	nd	nd	nd	nd	nd	nd
sum-naphthalenes(N)	74.3	59.5	24.2	124.0	124.7	26.9	134.7
sum-fluorenes(F)	12.0	11.3	3.8	24.6	22.6	25.6	23.4
sum-phenanthrenes/anthracenes(PA)	81.5	94.5	79.4	256.6	317.1	102.7	385.6
sum-dibenzothiophenes(D)	16.8	6.3	4.4	19.9	23.5	2.9	17.0
sum-fluoranthenes/pyrenes(FP)	15.5	24.6	9.1	27.1	36.7	9.2	33.2
sum-chrysenes(C)	17.8	18.1	6.6	33.3	46.5	7.1	33.4
sum-C20H12 aromatics(C20)	27.1	98.6	22.3	51.1	66.4	24.7	45.2
sum- 4,5 PAH (4,5 PAH)	59.6	134.8	34.8	108.4	149.4	38.7	107.3
sum-PAH(t-PAH)	252.6	319.4	152.0	552.5	654.5	201.4	682.6
N/PA	0.91	0.63	0.30	0.48	0.39	0.26	0.35
N/perylene	4.78	0.75	1.77	3.82	2.79	1.63	6.64
F/perylene	0.77	0.14	0.28	0.76	0.51	1.55	1.15
PA/perylene	5.24	1.18	5.80	7.90	7.09	6.23	19.00
FP/perylene	1.00	0.31	0.66	0.83	0.82	0.56	1.64
t-PAH/perylene	16.24	4.00	11.11	17.00	14.62	12.23	33.63

50

Table 11. (cont.)

Sample ID – UCLA No.	15	16	17	18	19	20	OS# µg/g dry wt
Surrogate Recovery (%)							
hexamethylbenzene	44	46	43.0	47	40	51	50
n-dodecylbenzene	63	59	50.0	58	59	56	61
4-terphenyl-D14	70	68	69.0	63	68	69	70
PAH (ng/g dry wt)							
naphthalene	nd	9.1	nd	9.6	1.3	0.5	2.9
C1-naphthalenes	nd	11.9	0.1	24.2	2.7	1.0	nd
2-methylnaphthalene	nd	8.7	0.1	12.1	1.5	0.5	nd
1-methylnaphthalene	nd	3.3	nd	12.0	1.2	0.5	4.8
C2-naphthalenes	nd	20.9	0.3	34.6	4.5	1.9	83.0
2,6-dimethylnaphthalene	nd	7.5	nd	10.0	1.4	0.4	31.0
C3-naphthalenes	4.9	7.7	0.3	26.2	4.3	1.4	44.2
2,3,5-trimethylnaphthalene	nd	nd	nd	4.5	0.8	nd	7.4
C4-naphthalenes	5.9	nd	nd	13.2	2.1	0.6	15.0
biphenyl	nd	4.8	0.1	5.4	0.8	0.3	nd
acenaphthylene	nd	nd	nd	nd	nd	nd	nd
acenaphthene	nd	nd	nd	nd	nd	nd	0.5
fluorene	nd	nd	nd	3.3	0.7	nd	1.5
2-methylfluorene	nd	nd	nd	2.7	0.4	nd	2.2
C1-fluorenes	2.7	nd	0.3	3.9	0.9	0.8	2.0
C2-fluorenes	8.5	nd	0.4	10.6	3.7	1.6	2.1
C3-fluorenes	tr	nd	tr	tr	tr	tr	nd
phenanthrene	10.3	17.1	1.0	18.3	3.6	1.9	2.3
1-methylphenanthrene	nd	3.7	nd	4.8	0.9	nd	1.1
anthracene	nd	nd	nd	nd	nd	nd	0.7
C1-phenanthrenes/anthracenes	86.7	25.3	15.0	124.1	24.2	109.3	3.8
C2-phenanthrenes/anthracenes	25.8	13.6	1.4	36.5	6.5	10.6	4.4
3,6-dimethylphenanthrene	nd	nd	nd	1.8	0.2	nd	0.3
C3-phenanthrenes/anthracenes	64.0	6.8	7.2	61.9	21.9	57.4	5.7
C4-phenanthrenes/anthracenes	13.5	nd	1.4	24.3	5.9	6.2	2.1
2,3-benzofluorene	1.4	nd	nd	1.3	nd	nd	nd
1,1'-binaphthalene	nd	nd	nd	nd	nd	nd	nd
d benzothiophene**	2.2	nd	0.2	2.8	0.5	0.3	nd
C1-dibenzothiophenes**	3.2	nd	0.3	3.5	0.7	0.6	0.4
C2-dibenzothiophenes**	3.2	nd	0.1	2.8	0.8	0.4	0.3
C3-dibenzothiophenes**	4.3	nd	tr	2.1	0.9	1.4	0.5
C4-dibenzothiophenes**	nd	nd	nd	nd	tr	nd	0.5
fluoranthene	2.4	2.6	0.2	3.2	1.8	0.7	2.5
pyrene	4.3	4.5	0.3	4.9	2.0	0.8	2.0
C1-fluoranthenes/pyrenes	4.5	0.9	0.1	5.6	1.0	0.7	0.9
C2-fluoranthenes/pyrenes	3.7	nd	0.3	5.2	0.8	1.2	1.1

PAH (ng/g dry wt) (cont.)	15	16	17	18	19	20	OS# µg/g dry wt
C3-fluoranthenes/pyrenes	1.5	nd	tr	2.4	0.6	0.3	1.1
C4-fluoranthenes/pyrenes	2.0	nd	nd	tr	0.7	0.2	1.4
benz(a)anthracene	0.8	4.8	0.1	1.6	0.4	nd	2.5
chrysene/triphenylene	6.8	10.2	0.3	9.9	3.7	1.3	2.8
C1-chrysenes/triphenylenes	6.1	6.6	0.1	10.5	4.3	0.7	1.6
C2-chrysenes/triphenylenes	2.5	nd	nd	2.0	5.3	0.4	2.4
C3-chrysenes/triphenylenes	nd	nd	nd	nd	1.1	nd	2.6
C4-chrysenes/triphenylenes	nd	nd	nd	nd	tr	nd	2.1
benzo(k)fluoranthene	0.8	nd	nd	0.7	0.4	nd	nd
benzo(b)fluoranthene	3.8	5.9	0.2	5.7	1.1	nd	nd
benzo(e)pyrene	4.5	nd	0.2	6.1	1.5	nd	nd
benzo(a)pyrene	nd	nd	nd	nd	nd	nd	nd
9,10-diphenylanthracene	nd	nd	nd	nd	nd	nd	nd
perylene	19.2	29.2	nd	18.8	4.8	1.1	nd
indeno(1,2,3-cd)pyrene	nd	nd	nd	nd	nd	nd	nd
d benz(a,h)anthracene	nd	nd	nd	nd	nd	nd	nd
picene	nd	nd	nd	nd	nd	nd	7.5
benzo(ghi)perylene	nd	nd	nd	5.3	nd	nd	nd
anthanthrene	nd	nd	nd	nd	nd	nd	nd
coronene	nd	nd	nd	nd	nd	nd	nd
1,2,4,5-d benzopyrene	nd	nd	nd	nd	nd	nd	nd
C1-C20H12 aromatics	4.2	tr	0.3	2.9	0.7	1.9	7.5
C2-C20H12 aromatics	nd	tr	nd	nd	tr	nd	4.1
C3-C20H12 aromatics	nd	nd	nd	nd	tr	nd	1.7
C4-C20H12 aromatics	nd	nd	nd	nd	nd	nd	nd
sum-naphthalenes(N)	10.9	49.6	0.7	107.8	14.8	5.3	145.0
sum-fluorenes(F)	11.2	nd	0.7	17.8	5.4	2.4	5.5
sum-phenanthrenes/anthracenes(PA)	200.3	62.8	26.0	265.0	62.2	185.5	19.0
sum-dibenzothiophenes(D)	12.8	nd	0.6	11.3	2.8	2.6	1.7
sum-fluoranthrenes/pyrenes(FP)	18.5	8.0	0.9	21.3	6.9	3.9	8.9
sum-chrysenes(C)	15.4	16.8	0.4	22.3	14.4	2.3	11.4
sum-C20H12 aromatics(C20)	32.5	35.2	0.7	34.1	8.5	3.8	13.3
sum-4,5 PAH (4,5 PAH)	62.9	64.7	1.9	76.4	29.5	7.4	22.8
sum-PAH(t-PAH)	303.7	181.9	30.3	493.2	116.3	206.1	207.9
N/PA	0.05	0.79	0.03	0.41	0.24	0.03	7.62
N/perylene	0.57	1.70	na	5.75	3.06	4.80	na
F/perylene	0.58	nd	na	0.95	1.11	2.14	na
PA/perylene	10.45	2.15	na	14.13	12.85	167.36	na
FP/perylene	0.96	0.27	na	1.13	1.43	3.54	na
t-PAH/perylene	15.84	6.22	na	26.30	24.01	185.96	na

51

Table 11. (cont.)

Surrogate Recovery (%) / PAH (ng/g dry wt)

Sample ID – UCLA No.	Pr. Blk	X-SPIKE 1	X-SPIKE 2	X-SPIKE Avg	Ref Sed SRM 1941†	NIST Values†
Surrogate Recovery (%)						
hexamethylbenzene	40	55	55	55	43	
n-dodecylbenzene	65	71	61	66	64	
4-terphenyl-D14	75	83	93	88	67	
PAH (ng/g dry wt)						
naphthalene	nd	34	30	32	1230	1322±14
C1-naphthalenes	nd			43		
2-methylnaphthalene	nd	44	40	42	336	406±36
1-methylnaphthalene	nd	43	45	44	214	229±19
C2-naphthalenes	nd			49		
2,6-dimethylnaphthalene	nd	50	48	49	237	198±23
C3-naphthalenes	nd			57		
2,3,5-trimethylnaphthalene	nd	59	55	57	87	96.3
C4-naphthalenes	nd			57		
biphenyl	nd	57	65	61	104	115±15
acenaphthylene	nd	58	60	59	106	115±10
acenaphthene	nd	57	53	55	46	52±2
fluorene	nd	57	59	58	88	104±5
2-methylfluorene	nd	80	76	78	61	73.7
C1-fluorenes	nd			78		
C2-fluorenes	nd			75		
C3-fluorenes	nd			75		
phenanthrene	nd	81	79	77	551	577±59
1-methylphenanthrene	nd	80	76	78	92	109±6
anthracene	nd	78	78	78	171	202±42
C1-phenanthrenes/anthracenes	nd			78		
C2-phenanthrenes/anthracenes	nd			75		
3,6-dimethylphenanthrene	nd	79	71	75	56	78.0
C3-phenanthrenes/anthracenes	nd			75		
C4-phenanthrenes/anthracenes	nd			75		
2,3-benzofluorene	nd	76	84	80	139	124.8
1,1'-binaphthalene	nd	70	82	76	98	117.0
dibenzothiophene**	nd	35	41	38	163	209.8
C1-dibenzothiophenes**	nd			78		
C2-dibenzothiophenes**	nd			75		
C3-dibenzothiophenes**	nd			75		
C4-dibenzothiophenes**	nd			75		
fluoranthene	nd	80	88	84	1132	1220±240

Sample ID – UCLA No.	Pr. Blk	X-SPIKE 1	X-SPIKE 2	X-SPIKE Avg	Ref Sed SRM 1941†	NIST Values†
PAH (ng/g dry wt) (cont.)						
pyrene	nd	78	86	82	970	1080±200
C1-fluoranthenes/pyrenes	nd			78		
C2-fluoranthenes/pyrenes	nd			75		
C3-fluoranthenes/pyrenes	nd			75		
C4-fluoranthenes/pyrenes	nd			75		
benz(a)anthracene	nd	59	63	61	449	550±79
chrysene/triphenylene	nd	88	84	86	622	641.0
C1-chrysenes/triphenylenes	nd			78		
C2-chrysenes/triphenylenes	nd			75		
C3-chrysenes/triphenylenes	nd			75		
C4-chrysenes/triphenylenes	nd			75		
benzo(k)fluoranthene	nd	61	67	64	386	444±49
benzo(b)fluoranthene	nd	74	74	74	712	780±19
benzo(e)pyrene	nd	68	60	64	534	573.0
benzo(a)pyrene	nd	56	62	59	56	670±130
9,10-diphenylanthracene	nd	77	74	76		
perylene	nd	68	62	65	39	422±33
indeno(1,2,3-cd)pyrene	nd	63	64	63	466	569±40
dibenz(a,h)anthracene	nd	62	60	61		
picene	nd	69	71	70		
benzo(ghi)perylene	nd	62	66	64	433	516±83
anthanthrene	nd	52	56	54		
coronene	nd	70	70	70		
1,2,4,5-dibenzopyrene	nd	58	66	62		
C1-C20H12 aromatics	nd			78		
C2-C20H12 aromatics	nd			75		
C3-C20H12 aromatics	nd			75		
C4-C20H12 aromatics	nd			75		

* Duplicate analysis
** Very low recovery due to activated copper treatment for sulfur removal
# OS=oil spill sample; note change in units of concentration
nd=not detected, below MDL
tr=trace amounts, not quantifiable
na=not applicable
% recovery of some methylated homologs assumed to be the same as that of methylated phenanthrenes

Table 12: Distribution (ng/g dry wt) of triterpenoids in gross sediments of Beaufort Lagoon. All sample numbers have the prefix BL03. O. is the oil spill sample.

SAMPLE ID – UCLA No. Triterpanes (ng/g dry wt)*	1	2	3	4	5B	6B	9	9B	10	11A
18α(H),21β(H)-22,29,30-trisnorhopane	tr#	tr	tr	tr	tr	2	1	1	1	1
17 α(H),21 β(H)-22,29,30-trisnorhopane	9	tr	6	tr	tr	6	4	3	1	3
17 β(H),21 β(H)-22,29,30-trisnorhopane	54	20	51	1	24	51	55	25	14	27
17 α(H),18α(H),21 β(H)-28,30-bisnorhopane	nd##	nd	nd	nd	nd	nd	nd	nd	nd	nd
17 α(H),21 β(H)-30-norhopane	16	10	20	1	11	22	18	11	2	13
17 β(H),21α(H)-30-norhopane	32	12	30	1	15	32	28	15	8	17
17 β(H),21 β(H)-30-norhopane**	138	37	111	2	61	125	128	39	33	39
18 α(H)-oleanane	nd	nd	nd	nd	nd	nd	nd	nd	nd	nd
17 α(H),21 β(H)-hopane	8	5	11	1	5	13	7	5	3	7
17 β(H),21α(H)-hopane	tr	9	nd	tr	16	tr	tr	27	tr	nd
17 β(H),21 β(H)-hopane	14	6	14	nd	7	14	12	6	3	8
22S-17 α(H),21 β(H)-30-homohopane	nd	nd	nd	nd	nd	nd	nd	nd	nd	nd
22R-17 α(H),21 β(H)-30-homohopane	tr	tr	tr	nd	nd	15	tr	nd	nd	nd
17 β(H),21 β(H)-30-homohopane	10	3	13	tr	6	13	8	6	2	5
22S-17 α(H),21 β(H)-30,31-bishomohopane	nd	nd	nd	nd	nd	nd	nd	nd	nd	nd
22R-17 α(H),21 β(H)-30,31-bishomohopane	nd	nd	tr	nd	nd	nd	nd	nd	nd	nd
22S-17 α(H),21 β(H)-30,31-trishomohopane	nd	nd	nd	nd	nd	nd	nd	nd	nd	nd
22R-17 α(H),21 β(H)-30,31-trishomohopane	nd	nd	nd	nd	nd	nd	nd	nd	nd	nd
22S-17 α(H),21 β(H)-30,31-tetrahomohopane	nd	nd	nd	nd	nd	nd	nd	nd	nd	nd
22R-17 α(H),21 β(H)-30,31-tetrahomohopane	nd	nd	nd	nd	nd	nd	nd	nd	nd	nd
hop-13(18)-ene	32	13	25	1	14	26	40	27	8	4
hop-21(22)-ene	nd	nd	nd	nd	nd	nd	nd	nd	nd	nd
diploptene	260	112	182	3	148	254	181	173	93	116

SAMPLE ID – UCLA No. Triterpanes (ng/g dry wt)*	12	13	14	15	16	17	18	19	20	OS µg/g dry wt
18α(H),21β(H)-22,29,30-trisnorhopane	1	3	1	3	nd	nd	1	1	nd	56
17 α(H),21 β(H)-22,29,30-trisnorhopane	6	8	5	4	13	nd	5	2	1	57
17 β(H),21 β(H)-22,29,30-trisnorhopane	44	32	36	16	202	nd	46	18	7	nd
17 α(H),18α(H),21 β(H)-28,30-bisnorhopane	nd	nd	nd	nd	nd	nd	nd	nd	nd	nd
17 α(H),21 β(H)-30-norhopane	24	23	23	15	57	1	19	8	2	315
17 β(H),21α(H)-30-norhopane	24	17	18	11	118	1	26	11	5	30
17 β(H),21 β(H)-30-norhopane**	87	70	83	29	398	1	107	45	13	56
18 α(H)-oleanane	nd	nd	nd	nd	nd	nd	nd	nd	nd	nd
17 α(H),21 β(H)-hopane	11	16	9	9	18	nd	8	3	1	263
17 β(H),21α(H)-hopane	tr	nd	nd	12	nd	nd	nd	nd	nd	nd
17 β(H),21 β(H)-hopane	13	11	10	2	44	nd	13	4	2	nd
22S-17 α(H),21 β(H)-30-homohopane	nd	nd	nd	nd	nd	nd	nd	nd	nd	103
22R-17 α(H),21 β(H)-30-homohopane	nd	6	nd	nd	nd	nd	nd	1	nd	68
17 β(H),21 β(H)-30-homohopane	11	6	9	3	11	nd	11	3	2	nd
22S-17 α(H),21 β(H)-30,31-bishomohopane	nd	nd	nd	nd	nd	nd	nd	nd	nd	44
22R-17 α(H),21 β(H)-30,31-bishomohopane	nd	nd	nd	nd	nd	nd	nd	nd	nd	31
22S-17 α(H),21 β(H)-30,31-trishomohopane	nd	nd	nd	nd	nd	nd	nd	nd	nd	27
22R-17 α(H),21 β(H)-30,31-trishomohopane	nd	nd	nd	nd	nd	nd	nd	nd	nd	7
22S-17 α(H),21 β(H)-30,31-tetrahomohopane	nd	nd	nd	nd	nd	nd	nd	nd	nd	7
22R-17 α(H),21 β(H)-30,31-tetrahomohopane	nd	nd	nd	nd	nd	nd	nd	nd	nd	Tr
hop-13(18)-ene	32	30	18	15	53	nd	21	9	2	?
hop-21(22)-ene	nd	nd	nd	nd	nd	nd	nd	nd	nd	nd
diploptene	352	211	314	143	903	1	184	64	28	nd

* Quantification based on m/z 191; also note change in the units for OS sample
** May be coeluting with C30 βα hopane in some samples
\# Trace amounts, not quantifiable   \#\# Not detected, below detection limits

Table 13: Distribution (ng/g dry wt) of steroids in gross sediments of Beaufort Lagoon. All sample numbers have the prefix BL03. OS is the oil spill sample.

Steranes (ng/g dry wt)*	UCLA No.	1	2	3	4	5B	6B	9	9B	10	11A	12	13	14	15	16	17	18	19	20	OS µg/g dry wt
5α(H)androstane		nd##	nd	nd	nd	nd	nd	nd	nd	nd	nd	nd	nd	nd	nd	nd	nd	nd	nd	nd	8
5α(H)pregnane		nd	nd	1.4	0.1	nd	nd	nd	nd	nd	nd	nd	1.5	0.8	nd	nd	nd	nd	nd	nd	8
5β(H)pregnane		nd	0.7	1.6	0.1	0.7	2.8	1.1	nd	nd	nd	1.4	4.2	1.9	2.1	nd	0.1	nd	0.7	nd	11
20-methyl-5α(H)pregnane		nd	nd	nd	0.2	0.4	1.0	nd	nd	nd	nd	0.9	1.7	1.4	nd	nd	0.1	0.8	nd	nd	4
20S-13β(H),17α(H)-diacholestane**	S1#	nd	nd	nd	0.3	0.8	3.7	1.0	0.9	nd	1.3	1.7	4.4	2.0	3.1	nd	0.1	1.7	0.9	0.5	116
20R-13β(H),17α(H)-diacholestane	S2	nd	nd	nd	0.2	0.7	2.3	0.7	0.9	nd	nd	1.8	2.6	1.3	1.8	nd	nd	1.0	0.6	0.2	92
20S-5α(H),14α(H),17α(H)-cholestane	S3	nd	nd	nd	0.2	0.8	2.6	1.1	1.0	nd	1.2	1.3	1.9	2.4	2.3	nd	0.1	1.5	0.8	nd	64
20R-5α(H),14α(H),17α(H)-cholestane	S6	nd	nd	nd	0.2	0.8	2.6	0.8	nd	nd	nd	1.7	2.9	1.7	nd	nd	nd	0.9	0.5	0.2	55
20R-5α(H),14β(H),17β(H)-cholestane	S4	nd	nd	nd	0.4	2.8	6.7	1.8	nd	nd	nd	4.2	6.6	3.4	nd	nd	nd	2.1	1.1	0.6	215
20S-5α(H),14β(H),17β(H)-cholestane	S5	nd	nd	nd	0.2	1.5	5.2	nd	nd	nd	3.3	2.3	3.9	1.8	nd	nd	nd	2.3	1.3	0.3	125
20R-24-ethyl-13β(H),17α(H)-diacholestane	S7	nd	nd	nd	0.2	1.2	3.2	1.8	nd	nd	nd	1.0	5.0	1.5	nd	nd	nd	1.1	0.5	0.2	170
20S-5α(H),14α(H),17α(H)-ergostane	S8	nd	nd	nd	nd	nd	nd	nd	nd	1.3	nd	nd	5.2	nd	nd	nd	nd	nd	nd	nd	37
20R-5α(H),14α(H),17α(H)-ergostane	S11	nd	nd	nd	0.2	nd	nd	2.5	nd	nd	nd	nd	7.5	1.3	nd	nd	nd	2.3	nd	nd	126
20R-5α(H),14β(H),17β(H)-ergostane	S9	nd	nd	nd	nd	nd	nd	nd	nd	nd	nd	5.5	4.3	nd	nd	nd	nd	1.9	nd	nd	217
20S-5α(H),14β(H),17β(H)-ergostane	S10	nd	nd	nd	0.2	nd	nd	nd	nd	nd	nd	nd	7.2	5.5	nd	nd	nd	nd	nd	nd	63
20S-5α(H),14α(H),17α(H)-stigmastane	S12	nd	nd	nd	0.2	nd	nd	nd	nd	nd	nd	nd	1.0	1.5	nd	nd	nd	nd	nd	nd	69
20R-5α(H),14α(H),17α(H)-stigmastane	S15	7.5	6.9	5.4	0.1	3.1	3.2	1.6	1.4	2.0	1.1	3.7	5.4	13.0	8.7	38.2	0.1	2.1	1.4	1.2	26
20R-5α(H),14β(H),17β(H)-stigmastane	S13	nd	nd	nd	0.3	0.8	2.3	1.5	nd	1.1	nd	3.2	3.0	2.4	nd	nd	nd	2.0	0.7	nd	141
20S-5α(H),14β(H),17β(H)-stigmastane	S14	nd	nd	nd	nd	nd	nd	nd	nd	nd	nd	nd	nd	nd	nd	nd	nd	nd	nd	nd	55

* Note change in the units for OS sample
** Steranes of similar configuration assumed to have the same RF as in the standard compounds mixture
\# Notation to be used in figures   ## Not detected, below detection limits

Table 14: Component loadings for the first two PCs.

Metal	Comp.1	Comp.2
V	0.338	0.120
Cr	0.311	0.131
Mn	0.116	-0.473
Ni	0.343	-0.106
Cu	0.335	0.010
Zn	0.316	0.260
As	0.269	0.074
Cd	0.242	-0.232
Sn	0.264	-0.387
Ba	0.162	0.434
Pb	0.338	-0.162
Fe	0.323	0.143

Table 15: Correlations between PC 1 and PC 2 with latitude, longitude, silt and organic carbon.

Parameter	PC 1 (p-value)	PC 2 (p-value)
Latitude	-0.544 (0.0160)	-0.304 (0.2058)
Longitude	0.021 (0.9324)	0.328 (0.1709)
Silt	-0.274 (0.2572)	0.758 (0.0002)
OC	0.547 (0.0153)	-0.242 (0.3173)

Table 16: Correlations between PC 1 and PC 2 with latitude, longitude, silt and organic carbon (excluding outliers BL03-4 and BL03-17).

Parameter	PC 1 (p-value)	PC (p-value)
Latitude	-0.428 (0.0862)	-0.473 (0.0551)
Longitude	0.147 (0.5742)	0.604 (0.0102)
Silt	-0.726 (0.0010)	0.516 (0.0339)
OC	0.516 (0.0341)	-0.390 (0.1218)

Table 17: Analysis of Variance for the Response of PC 1.

	Df	Sum of Sq	Mean Sq	F Value	Pr (F)
Silt	1	39.30097	39.30097	26.30329	0.000153386
Latitude	1	14.34431	14.34431	9.60034	0.007856686
residuals	14	20.91805	1.49415		

Table 18: Comparison of the mean concentrations of selected trace metals in Beaufort Lagoon mud with ERL and ERM guideline values, in percent incidence of biological effects in concentration ranges defined by two values as reported by Long et al. (1995).

| | THIS STUDY | Guidelines | | DATA FROM LONG ET AL. [1995] | | |
| | Beaufort Lagoon ppm dry wt | ERL | ERM | Percent (ratios) incidence of effects* | | |
		ppm dry wt		< ERL	ERL-ERM	>ERM
As	14	8.2	70	5.0 (2/40)	11.1 (8/73)	63.0 (17/27)
Cd	0	1.2	9.6	6.6 (7/106)	36.6 (32/87)	65.7 (44/67)
Cr	73	81	370	2.9 (3/102)	21.1 (15/71)	95.0 (19/20)
Cu	36	34	270	9.4 (6/64)	29.1 (32/110)	83.7 (36/43)
Pb	17	46.7	218	8.0 (7/87)	35.8 (29/81)	90.2 (37/41)
Ni	39	20.9	51.6	1.9 (1/54)	16.7 (8/48)	16.9 (10/59)
Zn	92	150	410	6.1 (6/99)	47.0 (31/66)	69.8 (37/53)
THg	0.04	0.15	0.71	8.3 (4/48)	23.5 (16/68)	42.3 (22/52)

* Number of data entries within each concentration range in which biological effects were observed divided by the total number of entries within each range.

56

Table 19: Comparison of the mean concentrations of selected hydrocarbons in Beaufort Lagoon gross sediments with ERL and ERM guideline values, and percent incidence of biological effects in concentration ranges defined by two values as reported by Long et al. (1995).

	THIS STUDY	DATA FROM LONG ET AL. [1995]				
	Beaufort Lagoon	Guidelines		Percent (ratios) incidence of effects*		
	ng g⁻¹ dry wt	ERL	ERM	<ERL	ERL-ERM	>ERM
		ppb dry wt				
naphthalene	6.00	160	2100	16.0 (4/25)	41.0 (16/39)	88.9 (24/27)
2-methylnaphthalene	12.40	70	670	12.5 (2/16)	73.3 (11/15)	100 (15/15)
acenaphthylene	nd	44	640	14.3 (1/7)	17.9 (5/28)	100 (9/9)
acenaphthene	nd	16	500	20.0 (3/15)	32.4 (11/34)	84.2 (16/19)
fluorene	2.18	19	540	27.3 (3/11)	36.5 (19/52)	86.7 (26/30)
phenanthrene	15.67	240	1500	18.5 (5/27)	46.2 (18/39)	90.3 (28/31)
anthracene	0.21	85.3	1100	25.0 (4/16)	44.2 (19/43)	85.2 (23/27)
fluoranthene	2.73	600	5100	20.6 (7/34)	63.6 (28/44)	92.3 (36/39)
pyrene	4.69	665	2600	17.2 (5/29)	53.1 (17/32)	87.5 (28/32)
benz(a)anthracene	1.80	261	1600	21.1 (4/19)	43.8 (14/32)	92.6 (25/27)
chrysene/triphenylene#	8.91	384	2800	19.0 (4/21)	45.0 (18/40)	88.5 (23/26)
benzo(a)pyrene	0.63	430	1600	10.3 (3/29)	63.0 (17/27)	80.0 (24/30)
dibenz(a,h)anthracene	nd, below MDL	63.4	260	11.5 (3/26)	54.5 (12/22)	66.7 (16/24)
Sum PAH	314.44	4022	44792	14.3 (3/21)	36.1 (13/36)	85.0 (17/20)

* Number of data entries within each concentration range in which biological effects were observed divided by the total number of entries within each range
# Reported as chrysene in the Long et al. study.